Endless Waves:
A Story of Grace

NANCY KRUITHOF O'FARRELL

ENDLESS WAVES: A STORY OF GRACE

iUniverse books may be ordered through booksellers or by contacting:

iUniverse
1663 Liberty Drive
Bloomington, IN 47403
www.iuniverse.com
1-800-Authors (1-800-288-4677)

ISBN: 978-1-4917-5179-4 (sc)
ISBN: 978-1-4917-5176-3 (hc)
ISBN: 978-1-4917-5172-5 (e)

Library of Congress Control Number: 2014919566

Printed in the United States of America.

iUniverse rev. date: 12/01/2014

Endless Waves:
A Story of Grace

To Tom and Alicia,
who first told me about grace
in a language I could understand

Contents

Foreword

Writing a book is never easy. It's an arduous calling, an ache that will not be soothed, a determination to give full voice to ideas or, in this case, to a life. Especially when the subject matter is as personal and painful as that described in *Endless Waves*, revisiting and recording a story takes enormous courage. It's amazing that a woman so filled with shame and self-loathing since childhood, whose only safety from horrific sexual abuse and pastoral exploitation was strong walls of self-protection, could step from behind that barricade and bare her soul. Nancy O'Farrell does so with grace, honesty, and eloquence.

Through more than twenty-three years of personal recovery and professional work, I've heard thousands of stories, and, by this point, rarely am I surprised. I'm still, though, regularly astounded by the evil in the world, especially as perpetrated by family members and clergy. Nancy's story of repeated sexual abuse in her home is sadly common. Even more so are the issues that allowed that abuse to thrive: parental addiction, abandonment, and attachment disruptions. Truly, the sins of the fathers are repeated generation to generation.

For me, clergy abuse is a different story. I cringe to read of Nancy's abuse by the pastoral leader at a Christian school and its devastating effects on an already shattered spirit. The idea that a pastor could systematically exploit a wounded young woman (actually many young women) never ceases to stir rage within. He wasn't some boundaryless clergyman who fell prey to the adoration of a female. "Pastor Bill" was a methodical predator who, with cunning and guile, isolated and controlled. Yet, somehow, through endless waves of grace, Nancy survived.

As a professional counselor, I react to the inadequacies and ignorance rampant in my field. Too many people had the opportunity to see Nancy's pain and intervene, yet they failed to notice or take action. And the one person who did, unbelievably bungled the intervention. I seethe at a counselor's insensitivity in sending a young abuse survivor alone to talk to a judge without preparation or advocacy. Still, Nancy identifies some positives of her time at the Christian school and has immense gratitude for the angels who helped her escape.

Nancy's book is aptly titled. Through endless waves of grace over many years, and with the gentle assistance of two clinical professionals, a loving God "*brought [her] back from captivity*" (Jeremiah 29:14a) and from the shackles of shame and self-hatred and the addictions required to keep those demons at bay. The story is heartbreaking and uplifting. Clearly, God continued to pursue this wounded, desperate woman and never stopped moving her toward healing. God showered her with endless waves of enough positive moments to keep hope alive.

Endless Waves is very practical. Rather than merely telling a horribly wonderful story, Nancy shares specific, detailed steps that aided her healing. Her lists of how to live intentionally, be kind to herself, and embrace her identity as a woman provide defined, measurable actions. The Counselor's Notes explain important concepts like shame, self-hatred, self-abuse, dissociation, the importance of support groups, and social intelligence.

Countless women will identify with Nancy's story and her laborious journey of healing. For those readers who are discouraged by the difficulty and extensiveness of the healing process, read *Endless Waves*. For those who have yet to fully lean into the journey, read Nancy's book and follow her example of relentless determination. For counselors, clergy, and others who want to know how to better come alongside those in Nancy's shoes, implement the ways that her helpers gently, truthfully, and patiently walked with her. For anyone in need of encouragement or courage, *Endless Waves* provides a healing testimony of a woman who refused to stay broken. I expect the grace of *Endless Waves* will wash over your heart, too.

Marnie C. Ferree, MA, LMFT
Director, Bethesda Workshops, Nashville, TN
www.bethesdaworkshops.org
Author, *No Stones: Women Redeemed from Sexual Addiction*
Editor, *Making Advances: A Comprehensive Guide
for Treating Female Sex and Love Addicts*

Preface

Like endless waves,
The grace of God rolls in
To meet the shore of human cries and need.
All those who sail,
Who launch upon this sea,
Will find their Pilot sure; they will succeed.

The first time I saw the Gulf of Mexico I was struck with the realization that God's grace is constantly rolling into our shores, just as the waves in the Gulf did. That summer was not a good time for me. Only a few days earlier, I had fled from a cult situation where I had been "used" for nearly six years. Peace was all I wanted, just enough inner peace to continue living; hope and joy were never even considered. Though I was only thirty-four, life already seemed futile, and I was convinced that I'd soon die by suicide. God and I were not exactly on friendly terms. My feelings for Him were not at all positive, and I was sure He didn't think much of me either.

Yet this thought suddenly intruded: the grace of God rolls in. Why? To meet our cries and need. For a very long time, my poem that is shown above did not register with my spirit, but during the last few years, I have found it to be true. God's grace has delivered me and brought me to a wonderful and safe harbor. Perhaps my story of abuse, broken relationships, and recovery will help other troubled survivors to find their own peace and safety.

Included in *Endless Waves* are five types of data to inform the readers where I was on my journey.

- Narration
  This is the story line, presenting the main events and important details.
- Counselor's Notes
  The explanations of what I was experiencing and why I had these problems will help the readers better understand my abuse and resulting issues.
- Journal Entries
  These descriptions of how I felt during the times of abuse and therapy show clear progress as the story develops. Because some entries are placed with a section of similar narration, not all are in consecutive order.
- Poems and Scriptures
  Each of the poems included was written with a specific purpose or at a specific time, which correlates with the event being recounted. All scriptures are from the King James Version unless otherwise noted.
- Waves of Grace
  These waves show how God was working in my life, usually with little or no awareness on my part. Only after months, or sometimes years, had passed did I finally see God's hand in a particular situation.

There are times in *Endless Waves* when I reveal details of my struggles that might make some people uncomfortable. Please know that these items are not only to inform readers of common battles among the abused but also to encourage those who struggle with these things. Recovery is possible.

While living the story, God's grace was very elusive, but from my present viewpoint, I can see His continuous torrents flooding my life even from the beginning. I have been redeemed by God's power and love.

Acknowledgments

Special thanks to Caronita, Christine, Jada, Marie, and Shannon, friends who proofed this work and helped bring clarity to its pages.

Deepest gratitude to Debby, who set up the accompanying website, and to Alicia, who again worked through the spiritual and relational issues with me.

I am especially grateful to Marnie Ferree, who took the time out of her extremely busy schedule to encourage a new author and sister in recovery.

Also, many thanks to the editing staff at iUniverse, who were so patient in working through the many details of *Endless Waves*.

Most of all, praise to Jesus, who, because of His sacrifice, has extended endless waves of God's grace—even to me.

1

Early Years
(Birth to Age Twenty-Eight)

Setup

Born and raised in Michigan, I was the youngest of four, with three older brothers. My parents were hardworking and intelligent. They encouraged us to excel in school and taught us to be independent and skilled in many practical areas. However, they were not warm, caring people. My dad, an alcoholic, was often drunk; my mom, trying to cope, was cold, unresponsive, and often very depressed. I never bonded with my parents or even felt loved or valued as a daughter, and I grew up without a sense of self.

I enjoyed elementary school and my teachers. This was a safe place, and I did well. The two-room school held students from kindergarten through eighth grade and had bookcases from which we were allowed to borrow. I enjoyed reading, especially animal stories, and could spend an entire evening lost in a story. Many nights I took a book to bed with me and continued to read under the covers with a flashlight.

Our dogs were the highlight of my life. I loved the beagles we usually had, and I always wanted to be outside with them. My youngest brother, Norm, and I played store and drove miniature tractors and farm equipment under the lilac bushes during hot summer days. We often played in the barn on rainy days, building forts with straw bales and sliding down the mows of hay.

However, when I was about six, one brother began sexually abusing me in the barn, so it was no longer a safe place to play. A couple of years later, another brother began molesting me, too. This abuse hurt and terrified me. Sometimes a neighbor boy would team up with my brother and chase me down. Even though I would run my heart out, they were faster and would always catch me and rape me. I was eight or nine when this began and about twelve when they stopped. It didn't take long to discover that there was no safe place anywhere. Now, I wonder why I never told anyone, but I suppose I had already learned not to expect help from adults. I was on my own. That feeling of aloneness hung on me for the next fifty years.

I thought parental bonding would have occurred very early in life, long before I could remember. Connections would have been made years before the abuse happened. Perhaps the abuse from age six to twelve cut off attachments already formed, or maybe all the chaos and stress already present prevented bonds from forming in the first place.

Responses

The puzzle was how something from so long ago could still have had such an effect on me. It was difficult to understand that the way I looked at people and events today was based on what happened more than fifty years ago. This was such scary, frightening stuff to talk or think about. I did a lot of things over the years to make the pain go away. Physical pain did help the inner anguish to lessen, briefly maybe, but it helped.

As a child I would sit in church, positive that everyone knew how bad I was to have done all these unspeakable sexual acts. If I could have acted "right," people might have had a better opinion of me, but I was rough. I got into fistfights in the church hall while waiting for catechism to begin. I asked too many controversial questions in Sunday school, and I refused to join the church at sixteen, when everyone else my age did. As a bad girl, I didn't fit the mold.

A Wave of Grace

I do realize the truth now: I was a troubled child. Relationships were confusing. Yet I was very interested in spiritual matters, even while young. When I was nine years old, I was allowed to choose any book or game as a gift for learning my Sunday school verse each week. I chose a Bible. No one I knew had personal devotions; in fact, I never heard it mentioned, but I read my Bible every day. God was preparing me for my life.

My maternal grandparents meant the world to me. They still farmed, had animals, and attended a friendly, loving, old-time Methodist church, which I loved. It was a happy time when I was allowed to spend the day at their house. My grandfather, especially, gave me some good attention. One spring he planted a pansy bed for me under the front living room window. I kept my eye on it all summer and never forgot his kindness. When I was visiting, he always took me to town with him and bought me an Eskimo pie, sometimes two if he forgot he had already bought me one. Every night he would spend thirty minutes kneeling by his bed and praying aloud. Sometimes I heard him mention my name. Then I knew I was special to him and that he loved me.

A Wave of Grace

My grandparents are probably the reason I made it through all of my experiences. They loved and valued me, prayed for me and, included me. My grandfather's prayers carried me until recently when I could place myself in God's care.

When I was about ten, my mom took Norm and me to stay with her parents. Our teacher drove around that way to pick us up for school. It was safe, and I was so happy to be there, but Norm was not glad about it and for some reason wanted to go back home. I had hoped we would always stay, and I was so disappointed when the visit lasted only a few days. We went back to the same nightmare. Nothing had changed.

Two years later, both of my grandparents died from cancer within a few months of each other. Because my mom had just had a broken pelvis from a car accident, I didn't get to see them much during the end. What a sad time that was for me! I still miss them terribly. I could never understand why God took them from me when they were the only ones who loved me, and I needed them so badly. I made a decision that lasted for over fifty years: I would never love anyone again.

My dad never raped me, as my brothers did, but when he was drunk and could catch me alone, he would fondle me. Occasionally, I accompanied him on errands. One time, when I was fourteen years old, he stopped at a bar and got so drunk that he staggered all the way to the car. Another man close by noticed his intoxication, guided him to the backseat, and instructed me to drive. I managed, I suppose because I had driven tractors for years.

High school was a shock. My class went from eight students in elementary school to over two hundred in ninth grade. I couldn't adjust quickly. In ninth grade, I nearly failed, but my grades gradually crept up until, as a senior, I made straight As again. Although I had three friends during these years, my social life was almost nonexistent. I began to dread school and felt very much an outsider.

The guidance counselor was concerned about my grades in ninth grade and about some social difficulty that I was experiencing. She had me in her office several times, and once I told her a little about what was happening at home. She sent me to a judge's home near school but didn't hint why I was sent there or even that it was a judge. I walked the several blocks by myself, and when I got there, I realized that I was expected to give an official report. Since I didn't dare do that, I denied everything. That closed the door to talk to the counselor anymore, so I had no one to help me during that time, in addition to being considered a liar. I began withdrawing in my mind, even as I sat with my body at a desk. Life was so stressful most of the time that I have few memories of that period. In my earlier years, I had relief at school but not anymore.

> **Counselor's Note: Coping with Trauma—Disassociation**
>
> When a child is exposed to abuse and trauma, her mind may detach from the overwhelming experience through out-of-body sensations of floating, flying, or drifting out to sea. This coping mechanism is called disassociation. When someone disassociates, reality dims and loses its influence on the person's body, mind, and spirit, and increases the chances of survival.
>
> While disassociation lessens the immediate impact of suffering and fear on abused children, it eventually becomes a barrier to healing. Disassociated children and adults find it difficult to identify their emotions and needs. Their detachment is often misunderstood as apathy, laziness, or even stupidity.

The following journal entry, written decades later during counseling, was an example of my disassociation. I wrote many entries in third person, particularly when describing events too painful to accept.

> *Who could she tell? She was afraid of one brother, who could be very cruel. A lot of conflict was in the house, but sometimes when she was outside, she put herself in dangerous situations, too. There was no safe place for her, and life was dangerous. She seldom knew who she was or where she fit in. She often felt like she wasn't anyone, not a person at all. It was a long time before she realized the truth.*

Little Red-Brick Building

During eleventh grade, withdrawing was not enough. I made my own place where I stayed more and more as time went on, an imaginary small red-brick building that became more real to me than any physical place. It was so low that I had to lie on my stomach. I could see out of the narrow slits of window near the top, but no one could see in. I did everything I had to do and went everywhere I had to go, but my mind and heart were in that building. I learned to be numb and to have no feelings, not even much physical pain. Several times, I scratched my leg with a pin until it bled, then brushed on an over-the-counter medicine designed to eliminate corns on feet. The liquid was strong and would eat into the flesh very quickly. This feeling of pain actually gave me some relief and helped me cope.

Counselor's Note: Coping with Trauma—Self-Harm

Survivors of abuse and trauma frequently injure or harm themselves through cutting or burning. While this self-abuse may seem cruel, it often serves as a release for emotional pain or a way to control their out-of-control feelings and experiences. Researchers have discovered that self-injury releases chemicals in the brain that can actually create feelings of euphoria or comfort. In his book *The Boy Who Was Raised as a Dog,* Dr. Bruce Perry describes cutting as a way to induce feelings of disassociation. He writes that self-injury releases natural opioids in the brain that can actually create feelings of numbness or comfort. Self-harm also creates the illusion of control, where the victim becomes the abuser. Parents of teens who cut sometimes react with fear and anger, not recognizing the complex reasons behind their child's actions.

Running Away

During Christmas vacation as a senior, I withdrew all the money I had earned from my bank account, stole my mother's car, and drove to upper Michigan and across US 2 to Montana, where my brother Norm was stationed with the air force. I don't remember what the specific problem was at the time. No one was abusing me anymore. When I got to the base gate, I realized that since my brother was in the service, there was nothing he could do to help me. He was stuck, and there was certainly no place for me to stay, so I turned around and drove back through Chicago into Lower Michigan. I was acquainted with a couple who had a children's radio Bible program, and I had taken Bible studies from them. Although I did not even know what I wanted, I thought these people might be able to help. I stopped at their place, but by the drawn shades and undisturbed snow, I knew they were not at home. For five days, I stayed in a sleazy but cheap motel and continued checking their house. Since they did not return, and I ran out of money, I drove to the home of one of my friends. The parents immediately called my mom, who came right over. The first thing she did was demand the car keys. She was angry, and I wouldn't talk to her or go home with her. The family where I was staying couldn't keep me, so I finally went to another friend's place and lived with them until the end of the school year.

A Wave of Grace

About a year later, the couple I had tried to contact to help me did become my friends. They were very touched by my situation and encouraged me for the next twenty years. Many pleasant weekends were spent with them.

My mom and I did reconcile the following summer, although we were never close. My running away was never discussed or even mentioned. It was the usual: sweep it under the rug to convince ourselves that it did not happen. We learned to get along, though, and to be pleasant with each other.

In my fifties, I also made peace with my two abusive brothers. Although we were not close, and I never desired to discuss the abuse with them, I was able to visit and enjoy my time in their homes. Both have visited me several times in my home and helped me with house projects. We were on friendly terms and expressed care toward each other.

I stuffed away all my feelings and spent more time in my little red building. Reinforced daily were the thoughts that I was nothing, no one, and was on my own to live or not live. Even though I had not heard much about suicide, it became an option that I considered more and more frequently.

The fall after graduation, I attended nursing school. The year was not good. I stayed isolated as much as possible. While the bulk of the first year was college courses, hospital floor work was gradually added. This was what frightened me. I had to deal with patients and personnel, even doctors occasionally, and one very stern supervisor who often told us that by the end of the year she would eliminate 50 percent of the class. I was also afraid of one of my patients, and one day I charted that I had done a procedure for him, when, in fact, I had not. This lying got me expelled.

Kicked Out

It was scary at the hospital, and there were so many situations to deal with, I just couldn't manage the work. I was slipping, going downhill, and didn't know where to turn. I was glad to be expelled. It was much too stressful. During that year, I didn't sleep much and brooded a lot.

When I was eighteen years old, I remember sitting at my desk in the nursing school dorm, feeling that something in my life was terribly amiss but having no inkling what it could be or where to get help. Even at that young age, I felt a cloud of gloom over my head. During that same night, I wrote the following dark poem:

Why I Always Leave
I pray, or often try,
But the angry silence always stops
    it in my mouth;
    and though I try again,
    it's not the same.
I've ignored Him too long,
    now all attempted conversation
    sours in my mouth.

I don't want people telling me
    all will be okay in time.
    It won't—I know.

Hopes just get raised
    then dashed to death again,
    though inwardly I cry for hope,
    for help,
    and for a human touch.

But those who are the closest
    I'm the most afraid of,
    afraid they will know me,
    then turn against.
Only a few I've let in
    and bared my soul a little, too,
    now and then,
    but then I have to leave.

I try to explain it all to God,
    tell Him how sorry I am
    for being what I am,
    doing what I do.
I try to tell Him how I feel,
    how I need His help.
    People say He's always with us.

I really don't want to die
    and yet so often I feel
    no other choice is given me
    die or die,
    whichever comes first.

It doesn't matter so much,
    not anymore—it's late.
    Everything is too big or too much,
    easier to just drop it all and go.

Call it anything you want,
    but it's hurt, just plain hurt,
    hurt so bad
    I can't speak or breathe.
That's what forces me to always leave.

It was time to get a full-time job. I liked older people and was hired by a nursing home to work days. The local hospital also hired me to work part-time in the late afternoons and early evenings to help with the dinner trays and kitchen cleanup. Although I enjoyed both jobs, and even though I was living with a great aunt at the time, I continued the downward trend.

After working for a few months at the nursing home, as I was putting out evening medications for the nurse, I slipped a full bottle of sleeping pills into my pocket. As soon as I returned to my aunt's place, I told her I was tired and was going to bed. I took the entire bottle of sleep medication. Nothing happened during the next hour so I got up, told my aunt I couldn't sleep and was going out, and went to the hospital job. We would set up trays and get everything ready for meals, but since it was a little early for dinner, we'd taken a short break. I sat down and immediately passed out. Sunday morning, three days later, I woke up in a hospital bed that had been placed near the nurses' station where they could watch me. I was bound in a straitjacket; I can only imagine what might have transpired during those three days. The nurses were kind, but I couldn't explain the turmoil inside me.

———~w°∘◉⟊◉⟊◉⟊∘°w———

A Wave of Grace
Only by the grace of God did I survive. Later I learned it
was a very close brush with death. Although at the time, I
was angry to awaken, now I am glad. At that time I was
given life; now I have been given an abundant life.

———~w°∘◉⟊◉⟊◉⟊∘°w———

I was sent to Chicago to live with a brother and his family. Location wasn't the problem. The problem was me, and I had to live with myself in Chicago too. I was nineteen. Being in a new place could have started a new chapter in my life, but it didn't. I had different activities; I met different people; I worked different jobs; but I was still the same.

Within a few days, my sister-in-law introduced me to a group comprised of young people from various churches in the area. The leaders were an older couple who loved us. Youth would go to their house and help put out mailings that announced what churches were hosting the films and the social events that were planned.

The couple was truly dedicated and interested in us. They prayed with us and were helpful and encouraging. I liked being part of the group and made some friends. I was working at a large bank downtown, which was enjoyable. I thought of King Saul and how a spirit would torment him at times with great anger (1 Samuel 19:9–10). Similarly, I was tormented with depression and a sense of hopelessness. Bible reading, prayer, and church didn't seem to touch it. No matter how much I worked for Him, I could never get His approval. When I was twelve, I had been saved at Vacation Bible School, but I always thought that I was a constant disappointment to God, and, as a result, I thought that He didn't like me very much.

Counselor's Note: Spiritual Disciplines

Prayer, Bible study, fasting, and worship are all avenues in which to experience God's presence and learn more about Him. Like physical exercise, these spiritual exercises are vital aspects of being spiritually healthy. For trauma survivors and people with chronic anxiety and depression, however, these spiritual practices can become a source of frustration. Many Christians expect the spiritual disciplines to cure their emotional pain and may conclude that God does not hear them or love them. True healing and recovery can only begin when the source of the pain is revealed and then treated with insight, understanding, grace, truth, and time.

———⁓ɷɷɷ———

A Wave of Grace
But God did save me. Our church didn't teach about a
personal relationship with Jesus, and the experience didn't
seem to insulate me from problems, but God knew I was
His even when I didn't know.

———⁓ɷɷɷ———

Psychiatric Hospitalizations

Why the care of these leaders was not enough for me, I don't know, but again I attempted suicide and again very nearly succeeded. This time, after being in a hospital's emergency room, I was transported to a psychiatric hospital where, for three months, I talked very little but tried to sort things out in my mind. I was put on medication, eventually released, and, for several months, had weekly appointments with a psychiatrist. He didn't ask me anything, wanting me to volunteer whatever was on my mind. I seldom could think of anything, so sometimes the whole hour went by and I hadn't said one word. After a few months, he committed me again and ordered shock treatments. An injection was given to render me unconscious, then a rubber wedge was placed in my mouth, and the shock was administered. The first two times this was done to me, the injection didn't put me out, and I fought the wedge being put in my mouth. From then on, I was given a larger dose. These treatments did help me forget a lot of the past, but my attitudes, outlooks, lack of communication skills, and inadequate social adjustment were still the same, as well as the tenuous connection with God.

An unfortunate side effect from the shock treatments lasted most of my life. When I was about to drop off to sleep, I'd sense the wedge being placed in my mouth and was instantly awake. I didn't sleep much, and, for some reason, thought sleeping pills were very harmful, so I began drinking enough in the evening to put me to sleep. Alcohol-induced sleep is not especially restful, but at least I had a few hours.

In my early twenties, some good was being put into my life, especially from the youth group and its leaders. My desire for God was strong, but I simply did not trust Him. Actually, I trusted no one and went along day after day, doing what I felt I had to do but with no heart. What involvement I had besides work was with church and other such activities. That did not get me out of the pit though, and no matter how much effort I exerted, I could not make the God-thing work. At the same time, I knew God was my only option. Somehow, I had to reach Him.

During this period, I wasn't the only one with problems. The entire world was in turmoil: the building of the Berlin wall, the Cuban missile crisis, the Vietnam War, and the assassinations of Dr. Martin Luther King, Jr. and President John F. Kennedy. A cultural revolution was occurring, too, with the Beatles and Woodstock.

However, I was barely aware of activities outside of myself. What was happening inside was so much more real to me. My inner turmoil was accelerating. The following poem describes the turmoil.

Whirlwind
Lonely, and the waters swirled,
Lonely, and the wind unfurled,
Round and round and round it went
Till flesh and blood and breath were spent.
Like a funnel whirl, and when it stops
All within the whirlwind drops.
It matters not, I seem so old,
If death would suddenly grow bold.

I was desperate for relief. I was always consumed by guilt because I never did enough. To me, God was a stern dictator, always demanding more. After all, He is worthy, isn't He? So how could I refuse Him? Experience had taught me, however, that no matter what I did, it never seemed to make any difference in my life, but I was still afraid to curtail any religious exercises. I did not understand how unbiblical my view of God was or that my so-called service proceeded from obligation instead of love.

Several addictions had a hold on me, and I felt shame and condemnation. I was not worthy to enter God's presence, and yet He required so much. I was in a dilemma. I had a lot of turmoil and could not rest. I went to meetings and prayed dozens of times for salvation, but God never seemed to accept me. I hated who I was and was sure God could change me if He wanted to, but He apparently left that up to me. I didn't have the power to change myself and couldn't understand why He didn't know that. The conclusion was always the same: if I worked harder for Him, He would be pleased and would help me.

At twenty-five years old, I began training with a missionary organization in the Northeast, but the director decided I was too withdrawn to work in this field. His decision was a huge blow to me. I could have applied to other organizations, but I didn't. I was too discouraged. Hundreds of times I thought, *What does God want?* To me, the Bible was a book of rules that I tried to follow. My constant failures brought more guilt, which, in turn, pushed me to even more service. The cycle was unending.

I took evening classes at Moody Bible Institute in Chicago. I taught Sunday school and visited the elderly. I attended Bible studies and volunteered. Every time the church doors were open, I was there. Religious activity was all I did besides my regular job at a bank in downtown Chicago. In my head, I knew heaven would not be the reward of my frenzied activity but to sit and do nothing was even more guilt producing. I was confused and frustrated; my mind was muddled and my thinking in turmoil. The poem that follows shows my frame of mind:

Nothing
    Total emptiness
Like everything emptied out,
    Vomited up,
Even the lungs and heart and stomach,
    All of it.
    Nothing left.

The skin is rubbed off,
    And the flesh.
Even the bones are withered
    And shrunken.
    All is gone,
All feelings, hopes, and dreams,
    Dead and dried.

The music of the soul,
  Even the soul.

  There's no going,
All is already long gone.
  There's no thought,
Nothing left to think about.
  All is dead.
  All is dead.
  All is dead.

Counselor's Note: When Counseling Hurts

There are times when trauma survivors go to counseling only to leave with more scars than before. Counselors who are uninformed about the nature of trauma and abuse may attempt to "treat" the victim with paradoxical, conflicting statements, such as "Rededicate yourself to God," "Trust God and read the Bible more," and "Just pray and you will be healed." For someone raised in church or in a Christian culture, these recommendations can sound similar to advice given to a chronic sinner, thief, or drunkard: "Connect to God, and you will be forgiven." Such statements trigger spiritual shame and inadequacy, or a feeling that healing is a simple, one-step process similar to forgiveness for sin. Many survivors already struggle with inadequacy and a deep sense of failure at not being able to pray or think their way out of traumatic pain. This spiritual shame is further compounded by the fact that many abusers use spiritual statements such as "God is ashamed of you now" to shame their victims, especially if the abusers hold positions of leadership in a church or ministry.

Another problem with prescribing spiritual practices to trauma survivors is that these wounded men and women have traumatized brains that cannot accurately interpret these messages. When someone experiences trauma, their rational, thinking brain, called the prefrontal cortex (PFC), goes dormant in order to allow the limbic system full power to initiate survival behaviors. The limbic system scans the environment for any sign of threat and then sends powerful chemicals into the blood stream to prepare that person to fight, flee, or freeze. Since the PFC is dormant, messages or information about abuse or healing are filtered

---

through the limbic system. Messages that imply that the trauma survivor should be doing something that they have already tried and failed at will be interpreted as shame messages similar to their abuser's taunts. It is likely that the victim's abuser has already shamed them with messages such was "It's your fault," or "God despises you now. He won't hear your prayers because you are disgusting," or "Go and pray now so God will forgive you." If spiritual shame is not addressed in a nurturing relationship, then the messages received from an uninformed counselor will only aggravate these shame wounds.

Trauma victims must experience safety and comfort in therapy for a long period of time before their limbic systems begin to calm down. It is only at this point, which may be months later, that the trauma survivor can accurately receive and interpret messages about healing and recovery. A therapeutic relationship filled with empathy and compassion provides trauma victims the opportunity to combat the inner core of shame and embrace their vulnerable selves with Grace.

2

Minnesota
(Age Twenty-Eight to Thirty-Four)

Abuse and Shame

When I was twenty-eight, the son of a friend learned about a small Bible school in Minnesota. Since I had tried so many avenues to get peace and hope in my life, I began to think that studying the Bible full time might be just what I needed, so I applied and was accepted

Without a doubt, this was the worst mistake of my life. So much spiritual damage resulted from this decision. Life, already on a downward spiral, now took a nose dive. Pastor Bill (his name has been changed) was the director of the school. Although he was fifty-three years old, he immediately took an interest in me. Since I had no concept of boundaries and healthy relationships, the concern he had for me was welcomed. Most students were younger than I and were housed in dorms. Because older students were given their own place, I didn't think much about being given my own mobile home. Later, I realized that I was the only single woman who was given a place for herself and discovered that it was right behind his house and office.

The daily life at the Bible school was a facade of normalcy. We awoke early and were encouraged to have personal Bible reading. Classes lasted from eight in the morning until noon, with the Bible as the only textbook. Most courses were books of the Bible with topics such as evangelism and missions. Pastors from various denominations would stay a week or two to teach, and often Pastor Bill or one of the upper-class students would teach. During the six years I was there, I taught seven different courses.

Because it was classified as a vocational school by the state, we had many on-the-job training opportunities. Friday evenings were often spent in a home at one of the nearby Native American reservations. The house would be packed with friends and neighbors. For our usual home meeting, we would have singing, testimonies, puppets, and a short message by a student. Then we'd split up and pray with individuals for salvation, healing, or any other need. Frequently, we'd go somewhere for a weekend, having Saturday with the children and youth and Sunday morning with the regular church service. Twice during each school year, we traveled to other states on two- or three-week tours.

This description sounds wonderful, but another story was also unfolding. Pastor Bill had coerced me into a sexual relationship. My official position, right from the start, was office assistant. I soon learned to do the layout for newsletters, to put out mailings, and to plan retreats and summer camps. Within two weeks, I was working several hours every evening. He soon dismissed his full-time secretary so he could approach me unhindered whenever he chose. From then on, I had little free time; Pastor Bill would include sex in my daily responsibilities. He would lock the doors and sexually force me. Pastor Bill had five grown children, some older than I was. Even though he carried on the illusion of marriage and the illusion of being a godly pastor, he had selected women before me and did again after me. Little did I know that I would be stuck in this exploitive relationship for nearly six years. The torment and the spiritual damage were astounding.

One consequence of abuse is that the victim assumes all or part of the blame, which causes huge amounts of shame. The following journal entry reveals how I took the blame for Pastor Bill's abuse:

> *Journal, May 28, 2009*
> *When I applied to the school, I didn't realize that God was willing to guide me in the right path. All I had to do was ask Him, but I didn't. After all, Bible school sounded like a good thing. How could something so good turn out to be so bad? I was an idiot and sickening even to myself. What*

a disappointment I must have been to God! In the same old pit! Like the Bible says, "A sow to its wallow or a dog to its vomit" (2 Peter 2:22).

Only later did I think of this situation differently. How would I have known Pastor Bill was wielding control instead of care? Males in my family treated me the same way in my growing-up years. He had the position of authority as pastor and was twenty-five years older than I. He was a former military man and had a very commanding presence. In addition, I had never learned about boundaries. The early abuse taught me that I was powerless with no voice, and people should be allowed to do whatever they want with me.

I received a great amount of head knowledge, but, because of my shame relationship with the director, I had to shut off my heart. Therefore, the scripture, which is meant to reach the heart, never did reach mine. Even though I learned to prepare and deliver a testimony, it felt fake because of my secrets. The same applied to whatever I did to present the Gospel. It all seemed artificial to me, as if my real life were living for Pastor Bill, not for God. It took me a long time to understand that I had had no choice when it came to Pastor Bill and his sexual expectations.

Crushed

Pastor Bill's car would be parked in his garage, and I would often be required to climb into the trunk and ride undetected until well out of town. We would go somewhere for a day or two. Not only was the sexual obligation horrendous but also the rest of the time when I had to act like everything was normal, as if nothing was wrong. I was just pretending—an actor who played a part! I wasn't real at all. I not only had to do the part, but I also had to enjoy it. I had to act like I wanted to do this, yet, at the same time, I was positive that it was the "wanting to" that would send me to hell. Pastor Bill was able to read my mind, so I had to do more than pretend—I really and truly had to enjoy it. But I hated the life I was living, and I despised what I had become. I had to push down those thoughts and feelings to the point where I no longer felt or cared.

Pastor Bill bought whatever I needed; he made sure that he provided everything until I was totally dependent on him. If everyone went out somewhere, he'd slip me a little cash. I didn't get paid for my office work, but I never dared ask since I didn't pay to live there or to attend school as everyone else did. Now I see it as part of his plan to keep me there.

Counselor's Note: The Power of Betrayal

Patrick Carnes outlines the five avenues of betrayal in his book *The Betrayal Bond: Breaking Free of Exploitive Relationships*. Betrayal by seduction, terror, power, intimacy, and spirit all create a sense of fear and dependence on the abuser. Betrayal by a supervisor and spiritual leader is one of the most powerful and overwhelming traumas a woman can experience. Should she have rebelled against his authority, a woman caught in this trap risked being fired, exposed as an adulteress, abandoned without provision, and possibly physically harmed. Escaping a trauma bond takes extreme courage to risk not only being attacked by the abuser but also shamed by those who fail to recognize the trap that trauma bonds create.

Pastor Bill's wife worked at the local newspaper shop. Wednesday was printing day so she'd be gone all day. Pastor Bill would cook for me; I would have to help him and enjoy eating with him. After the demanded intimacy, he ordered me to go to sleep there in his arms. I was terrified but had to pretend to nap for a few minutes. I detested Wednesdays. To shut down a part of myself was necessary, not just making it nonoperational, but actually shutting down a large part of my mind.

The hours when I would teach and stand in front of the students, knowing where I had just been, brought relentless condemnation. My constant thought was, *The Bible teacher is just an acting part. I am actually a damn slut!* During church services, when a few people from the community came, my feelings were much more intense. They were mostly friends of Pastor Bill's wife, probably there to lend support to her. They all knew what was going on; I knew they knew, and they even knew that. Yet, all had to be fine, not just acting fine, but truly fine. Having to be an upstanding Christian leader and example, which I could not conceive being, brought enormous amounts of guilt and shame. And getting forced into what I abhorred somehow became intertwined with church and God.

Many years later, during counseling, I often relived the situation. My harsh condemnation of myself would shut me down, until I could express my distress only by using the third person. This is what I wrote one day:

> *It's impossible to describe fully the horrible condemnation every time she stood in front of a class, knowing that every word she taught was bringing further damnation, knowing that every time she would again submit to Pastor Bill, she would be reinforcing the certainty of hell. Then she had to convince herself that she truly enjoyed it all. After a while, she didn't cry anymore at night. She had been crushed.*

A Wave of Grace

Pilate asked Jesus, "What is truth?" (John 18:38); I had to confront the same question. I had to release the lies I previously believed and accept the truth. Pastor Bill's assaults, intimidations, and threats introduced tremendous trauma into my body, mind, and spirit. I was viciously trapped by the premeditated schemes of a sexual predator.

A Caged Rat

Even though humiliation and shame filled me all the time, my not being able to show or express these emotions warped my spirit. Forced to do all that was expected, while being open and jovial, twisted my very soul, making any relationship with God or others impossible. I often had to separate: a part of me always did what had to be done, but I stayed in my imaginary brick building where it was safe. I must have become a nonperson (if I wasn't already), because later, it didn't matter what was done to me, which actually made it easier for me to get through the day.

On six different occasions during these years, I worked up my courage and expressed the desire to stop the sexual relationship. Pastor Bill would always agree. Then he would refuse to speak to me, not one word. At the same time, however, I was still responsible for my work but got no feedback from him. He refused to acknowledge me, for weeks sometimes, until I again submitted to him. Then all was back to the same: sex with the work. He lectured me a lot about total submission, often telling me that submitting to him was the same as submitting to God, since he was God's representative here. He always won.

> *Journal, June 6, 2009*
> *Even while writing this thirty years later, I often covered my face out of shame! I don't know how I lived through it. I can understand how huge groups who are following someone could commit suicide. After all this time, it still makes me so afraid.*

I was not only Pastor Bill's sex slave but also his mind slave. I felt like an absolute fool, very humiliated, like Hester Prynne in *The Scarlet Letter*, but since I had to perform, I just pushed the feelings and emotions in a box. I could no longer discern what was spiritually genuine in myself and what was put on. The put-on became so real and what was truly real seemed put on, until I couldn't distinguish which was which. Many years passed before this dilemma changed.

So much of the time I was involved in spiritual activities. We would conduct meetings, witness on the streets, sing, and give testimonies. What was real then and what wasn't? I thought to myself, *Is there anything of God in me, or is it all make believe?* I couldn't tell. And, even long afterward, when I went to the altar at church, I couldn't determine if I was sincere and genuine, or if I was just acting. It was all very fuzzy. These thoughts continued to haunt me for the next thirty years.

Sometimes I would revert to my alcohol habit, always in my own house, but Pastor Bill knew, for he would often call me to come to his office in the evening, or he might come to me. Once when I tried to stop his sexual advances, I used Galatians 5:19 as my evidence, where it says that those who commit sexual sins will not enter the kingdom of heaven.

His reply? He said, "It says drunkenness too," and since I drank, what right did I have to speak of his behavior? I was a caged rat for six years.

Terror, Too

One time, when I disagreed with Pastor Bill, he took my hand and gradually, as if just toying with me, pulled back a finger. He didn't say anything, did not appear angry, and seemed very cool. When my finger broke, he dropped my hand but still didn't say anything. It scared me; I didn't know what I was supposed to do and didn't dare to respond. It was an important lesson, and I never forgot it. Pastor Bill would kill me anytime he wanted to if I ever became more useful to him dead than alive. From then until I was able to escape, terror was added to the shame and condemnation.

Many, many times his mere look would take my breath away. Usually I wouldn't even know why he gave me that look. I would frantically rack my brain to come up with something that caused it, something I was supposed to have done. The cause was often irrational; there was no way I could have known, yet I was responsible for taking care of it.

Even on our extended trips, Pastor Bill didn't limit his power over me. Two or more students would room together with volunteer families, but he would arrange for me to stay alone so he could pick me up and continue his sexual manipulation. Here we were, ministering in churches and schools, youth groups and nursing homes, preaching and praying with people. None of this seemed to make any difference in Pastor Bill's behavior. We had a limousine, and on trips he would make me sit up front with him. Early one morning when the team was on the road and everyone was supposedly sleeping in the limo while he was driving, he casually covered the two of us with a blanket, took my hand, and put it on him, right there in the filled vehicle. I had better not hesitate or express dislike in any way. Later, I was in charge of this same group, knowing full well that some of them must have realized what had gone on, and if no one else knew, I certainly did.

So many times, I tried to pray about this horrible situation, but to me the prayers just sounded as if I were trying to excuse myself. The only response I could imagine that God would say was, "There's no excuse," and I really didn't think there was. All I could pray was, "Oh, God, have mercy." There was nothing else for me to say.

Tapes

Those years in Minnesota reinforced many tapes already in my head:

- Don't be close to anyone.
- All people are dangerous.
- Walls will keep me safe.
- I'm a disappointment to God.

A lot of new tapes were added:

- I am evil.
- There is no hope for me.
- God must hate me.
- I'm just a drunk and slut.
- God's promises don't apply to me.

A Wave of Grace
No longer do I believe any of these lies from the devil, the father of lies (John 8:44). These thoughts were not from God. Learning to surrender my ideas was a long process that required much support and encouragement from strong Christians. Eventually, I was able to believe what God says. This brought much relief and peace to my heart.

Under the heavy weight of guilt and shame, I could not seem to understand grace or get assurance of salvation. I worked for God even though I knew it would do no good, since salvation is not earned (Ephesians 2:8–9). I had faith for others and was confident that God loved them and that they could have forgiveness and eternal life, but it was not available for me. I believed I had had my chance but had forfeited it

I was convinced that Pastor Bill's compulsive abuse somehow was my sin. Teaching in front of those who knew the relationship was humiliating, oh yes, but much more than that, knowing God was looking at me filled me with shame and disgust. I already hated myself since my brothers had molested me, and I already was so angry because I was stuck with myself. In Minnesota, these feelings were multiplied exponentially. Since they were much too powerful for me to manage, I buried them. It was much better to feel nothing, to be numb, and to isolate.

A Wave of Grace

The shame and guilt did eventually leave. Praise God! By continuing to put myself under loving people and sound teaching, God's truth pressed through all my false beliefs and brought me into His light. God helped me pursue Him and not quit, like Caleb, who at eighty-five years old affirmed his strength to still fight and conquer (Joshua 14:10–12).

Escape

After nearly six years, a miracle happened. All the students and Pastor Bill were planning a three-week tour to western states. Even though I had always gone on every previous trip, Pastor Bill decided I needed to stay at school to catch up on office work and begin making summer plans. This, I was soon to learn, was a God-act.

About a week after the team left, I made an appointment to talk with a local pastor about my dilemma. Although I tried my best to disguise the information I gave, he saw through it and said, "You're talking about Pastor Bill and yourself. You can do only one thing: leave." Up until that moment, the thought of flight had not even occurred to me. After all, I was a slave. It was providential that I had not actually thought of it before everyone left, because Pastor Bill could read my mind, and I would not have been allowed to remain. Although the possibility of escape was so hard to believe, because I thought I would die there, as soon as the pastor presented the opening to leave, I knew it was my chance.

Immediately I began preparations. I had no money of my own. I had kept in touch with the same couple I had tried to contact when I ran away at seventeen. We were good friends now, and I asked them for a loan that they immediately wired to a nearby bank. I had a trailer hitch installed on my car, rented a trailer, and sorted and packed what I was able to haul. A lot of time also had to be spent in the office because Pastor Bill would call frequently to check on me and my work. The day before the group was to return I pulled out of town.

Somehow, before I left, I worked up enough nerve to call the state superintendent of vocational schools and report Pastor Bill's sexual abuse. The superintendent visited me, asking many questions. He furthered his investigation, and a few months after I left, the school was shut down by the state.

Counselor's Note: Rescuer

The Karpman Triangle, created by Stephen Karpman in 1968, is a therapy tool used by psychologists and counselors to explore the dysfunctional relationships between controllers, victims, and rescuers. As Patrick Carnes described in his book *The Betrayal Bond: Breaking Free of Exploitive Relationships*, controllers and their victims have a fused, addicted relationship that defies logic. Anyone who attempts to rescue the victim may be perceived as an enemy to the complex agreement between controller and victim. The only way for a victim to be rescued from the grip of an abuser is for the victim to rescue herself. This courageous act frees the victim from her mental prison and secures her future outside of the controller's power.

———ᴍᴡᴏᴏᴄᴇᴛᴏᴏᴛᴇᴏᴏᴍ———

A Wave of Grace

Many waves came rolling in during the last weeks at the school:

- *I was left behind by myself.*
- *My escape had not occurred to me before the group left.*
- *The pastor I talked with had the courage to tell me the truth.*
- *The Holy Spirit placed the word of that man deeply in my heart.*
- *Friends sent me needed money.*
- *The team did not return earlier than planned.*
- *Although the two weeks I was preparing to leave were nerve-wracking, all went according to schedule.*

One more wave came later:

- *The school was closed forever. No other student would be forced to suffer abuse from Pastor Bill's hands.*

———ᴍᴡᴏᴏᴄᴇᴛᴏᴏᴛᴇᴏᴏᴍ———

I drove to Chicago, to the leaders of the youth group I had been involved with earlier. I told them I had left the school because of some actions there that I considered unethical. They said I could have a job with nominal pay and live with them. I unloaded the trailer and planned to stay. Because a team from the school had been there the previous year, Pastor Bill guessed where I might have gone and phoned the next day. This was before caller ID; when I answered, he asked me why I left. I told him the obvious: our sexual relationship.

Pastor Bill responded immediately with this verse, "No man, having put his hand to the plow and looking back is fit for the kingdom of God" (Luke 9:62).

Well, no news there! I already knew I wasn't fit for God, but He gave me this reply to Pastor Bill, "I don't know about that, but Joseph ran" (Genesis 39:12). And I hung up.

The call terrified me. He knew where I was, and I knew beyond any doubt that if he drove to Chicago and told me to get in his car, I would, and I would never get another chance to leave. My hosts were out for the evening, so I packed a suitcase and fled again.

3

Alabama
(Age Thirty-Four to Sixty-Three)

A New Job

Some friends had recently moved to Alabama, and, since that was far from Chicago, it sounded like a good place to be. When I got close, I called them; they welcomed me warmly. That evening, I explained a little of my situation to them, and I'm glad I did, for a few days later Pastor Bill called them. The family had had a team one time in their church in Illinois, and with the address change, Pastor Bill was able to track them. I will always be grateful to the dad for his outright lies: no, he hadn't seen me; no, he hadn't heard from me; no, he didn't know where I was. I was sitting right in front of him at the time, and if there was another call, the dad never told me. I lived with them for a few weeks, and, after getting a job at a chemical plant, I rented a place with other friends I had met.

I had been in Alabama for about a year when I decided to visit family and friends. As I was leaving for Michigan and Chicago, a friend who was a Christian teacher told me there were job openings at her school, but I replied that I was not interested and that I might be moving back up north. In Chicago, I applied for a position at a church, and while waiting to hear from that job, I visited my mom in Michigan. When a call came saying I did not get the job, my first thought was, *Good, now I can teach at the Christian school.* Since I had never given a conscious thought to that position, it totally surprised me. However, I was so positive about it, that when I returned to the chemical company where I worked, I turned in my resignation even before applying at the school. Although I heard nothing until a week before school began, I never doubted. It didn't occur to me that this was God working in my life. Besides not having much spiritual awareness, I assumed that God had certainly crossed me off. I was finally called in for an interview, of which I don't remember anything, but was later told that, as I walked out of the principal's office, the assistant principal walked in and told him that she didn't know who was just in, but that God had told her that person was to be hired. So I was!

—————

A Wave of Grace
I am so glad that I had friends who had moved as far away
as Alabama and that they welcomed me and covered for me.
They have been such a blessing in my life.

—————

Addictions

Meanwhile, I had many personal problems. I had been drinking heavily off and on for fifteen years, and although I had gone through detox and a substance-abuse recovery program the spring before, I still drank some to sleep and before social events. I continued other addictions I had developed to either punish or soothe myself: whipping my back, cutting, bulimia, and masturbation. People meant nothing to me. It wasn't that I didn't care, but I just couldn't connect. I had little idea what I was, not even realizing I was a *who*. In addition, I had few social skills. Nevertheless, I discovered that I was a wonderful teacher, intuitive and vibrant. I was completely different with children. I could relate to them, while being cool and indifferent with most adults. Although the school was a wonderful environment with caring teachers, my walls were so thick and high that I made little progress for many years. I seemed stuck where I was, neither getting much better nor getting much worse.

Many times, I wanted to just take off and leave, but I always held back. I knew I would still be with the main one from whom I wanted to escape—me. Every day, I thought of suicide, the only real escape.

I tried to live the way I thought was right. I helped others but never with my heart. Almost everyone, teachers and parents alike, were supportive and thoughtful, although I never understood why. It always surprised me. I was blessed by the years at this school. So many were friendly, but I couldn't get my heart open to let them in, and I had not yet learned to be a friend to myself.

─── ⁓⊙⊙⋇⊙⊙⋇⊙⊙⁓ ───

A Wave of Grace

What a tremendous blessing to be teaching side-by-side with so many wonderful people. I was amazed to be hired. Each time I was handed a contract for the next year, it surprised me, even though I was always highly commended by my supervisor and I had a list of parents wanting their children in my class. The compliments hit my armor and bounced off. Now I have finally learned to receive affirmations.

─── ⁓⊙⊙⋇⊙⊙⋇⊙⊙⁓ ───

Although I had a high IQ, my social ineptness "dumbed me down." Unless I was with only one other person, I was a social misfit. In a group, I felt lost. Even with only a few others, I couldn't find my place. I felt panicky and withdrew emotionally. I could present a prepared talk and could even joke, but I was only minimally present. People still scared me, no longer a fear-for-my-life scare, but I was never sure what could be said or done, so I couldn't prepare myself to respond. It was vital for me to have time to plan a response because I was so socially inadequate.

Teaching

In the classroom setting, I did quite well. I was formal with most parents, performing satisfactorily from my position. With the students, I generally had no problem and usually functioned much better during the school year than in the summer.

The main reason kids liked my class, I think, is because I put forth great effort to make the work interesting. We had science experiments, spelling bees, and an occasional day for comics in reading class. For all the subjects, we played a huge variety of review games. Art and board work were incorporated into every subject. Almost every day we did one especially fun activity. It might be a three-minute mystery to solve, group work to compose a Thanksgiving play, or a tic-tac-toe tournament. Many lively discussions had kids frantically waving their arms, nearly jumping out of their seats, anxious to have their say. My supervisor often commented on the intense interest and involvement of my students.

Every year I read aloud six to ten books. We went as a class to the school library, but since I wanted the students to enjoy books as much as I did, I scoured thrift stores and yard sales until our own classroom library had over a thousand books. Sometimes I'd read just a short section of one to get the children interested in a particular author.

The classroom had things to look at, too. Our wide windowsills were perfect for green plants, flowers, and unusual objects to make the kids curious. I had a huge collection of shells and rocks. We often had a class pet: a litter-box-trained rabbit, zebra finches, hamsters, etc. The cage would be cleaned on Friday, needed supplies would be bagged, and some fortunate child could take the pet home for the weekend.

I always looked for jokes that pertained to our subject matter and was very animated with my classes. One yearbook had a picture of several of my students laughing. The caption was, "How does Miss Kruithof keep her kids so happy?"

Counselor's Note: Safe Place, Safe People

Children and adults from traumatic backgrounds who find solace and comfort in a person or place often recover more quickly than those who are isolated. School can be a positive reinforcing environment, full of activity, color, games, and goals. Activities, such as sports, music, educational clubs, and volunteering with animal rescue can help relieve the pain and isolation of trauma.

The students were kept busy, and I walked around the room a lot. Probably three-fourths of the day, I was actively teaching, and one-fourth of the time I was giving individual help during practice sessions. This took care of most discipline problems.

I kept every card, note, and piece of artwork received from the students and parents. Those three boxes of memories tell many wonderful stories. Almost all the parents sent notes during the year about how grateful they were for me:

"Our whole family is blessed to have you as Matt's teacher."

"Thank you for all you do for Teresa. Your encouragement is why she is doing so much better this year."

"We love you and pray for you and the class every morning. This is the best school year Hope has ever had."

During the thirty-three years at the Christian school, I taught grades four through eight. Teaching was not difficult for me; the kids and books were my life. I was very accomplished in the classroom, although this vivacity did not carry over to any other area. Walking down the school hallways, I seemed so short, maybe a foot tall. Often I thought, *Why can't I just disappear altogether?* The rest of my life was nearly blank. Outside of school, I was entirely different: I was nothing. I have so few memories of those years. There were periods when my life went along quite evenly. By my fortieth birthday, I had completely stopped drinking and was active in church. Two things, however, did not change: my style of relating to adults and how I viewed God, others, and myself. This constant thought was uppermost in my mind: *Who am I to stand in front of these kids? They are better than I am. I'm just a wicked influence in their lives.*

I had daily Bible class in school and led many of my students to Christ, and I was able to integrate God's love and care into all the subjects. But I had no close relationship with God. I was merely working for Him. Although *grace* was a word I taught, it had never been a concept in my life.

"Mob, Be Gone"

Even though outwardly I was adjusting quite well, the least little thing that happened made me angry with myself. I had a lot of names to call myself, all very derogatory. It didn't really matter if I was at fault or not; I always blamed myself and my stupidity. Yet lots of people seemed to like me. I just didn't like myself. Truthfully, I did not know what they could see to like, since I did not seem to be very interesting and I did not connect well. For many years, there was not one person, other than my students, who really mattered to me.

During one especially rough time, in my middle forties, I began having tormenting nightmares night after night. A lack of sleep always exasperated my depression, so I was not doing well at all. Some friends at school got together and decided to take me to the local mental health facility to receive help. Although Susan [her name has been changed], my therapist, was wonderful, I couldn't seem to talk much. When she would ask a question, the voices in my head would argue back and forth, and I wouldn't know what to answer. Sometimes, if the arguing went on long enough, I wouldn't even remember the question. In addition, I had a large mass of voices that I called *the mob* that would prevent me from working on my basic problems. Whenever Susan would touch on one of these issues, the mob would continually scream, "*Danger, danger, danger,*" until I pulled back from the topic. The mob was similar to a guard dog that would prevent a child from approaching a busy street.

Often I sat for thirty minutes without saying a word. I was aware that I wasn't talking and actually felt pretty stupid just sitting there, but I couldn't think of anything to say or answer. Susan was a Christian but was not allowed, nor had she received the training, to give biblical counseling. I had always felt that my basic problems were spiritual, but I also realized that religious activities had never helped. In fact, I was gradually going down. Susan worked with me for several years. During one session when the mob was being especially vocal, she quietly spoke to it, "*Mob, be gone!*" Instantly the mob disappeared and never did return. That was very astonishing to me; my inside was much quieter.

> **Counselor's Note: The Mob**
>
> Nancy's description of *the mob* may be interpreted in several ways, depending on the person doing the interpreting. A mental health professional may call the mob a hallucination and want to prescribe medication. A minister may call the mob spiritual oppression and want to perform an exorcism. Without a discerning approach, some well-intentioned pastors may retraumatize trauma victims by addressing psychotic symptoms with exorcism. Fortunately, Nancy was not labeled as psychotic or demon possessed. Her therapist treated her with respect while also addressing the distressing symptom in a spiritual way.

This was not the first time the demonic oppression was addressed. Once, when I was twenty-six years old, a pastor took his belt and tried to whip it out of me; I soon fainted. Another counselor tried to cast out a "mute demon" because of my reluctance and apparent inability to talk. My quietness, however, was a result of the trauma and distrust. Susan was different. She approached the problem with calmness and consideration for me.

It would be reasonable to think that after the roaring mob was gone, I must have made much faster progress, but I didn't. The danger part was so ingrained in me that I continued to think of it even though there were no longer any voices. Eventually, individual therapy was phased out, leaving only group therapy. Since I was doing better, and Susan did not think group therapy would be beneficial for me, I dropped out.

A Blessing

Three or four years later, one of my room parents asked if I wanted to meet someone. I was fifty-five years old by this time and had never been particularly anxious to date, but I told her I would meet him. Wayne contacted me that evening, and we met the next day.

Wayne O'Farrell was fifty-three and a native Alabamian. He was charming, outgoing, and very funny. From the first date, we saw each other almost every day.

Wayne tried to keep me more updated with local and world events. I was teaching seventh grade when Mount St. Helens erupted and during the launching of the Hubble telescope into space. Events such as these helped the students see how vital science was. Wayne told me about the panic some of his coworkers felt when Y2K approached and the astounding amount of supplies they had stockpiled. He was very knowledgeable about history and taught me a lot.

Because Wayne's delivery doctor had mishandled him, he suffered a stroke as a newborn, and as a result, was legally blind from birth. He also had little use of his left arm and hand. All his life, he could have received disability, but he chose to work. For over thirty-one years, he helped to keep the grounds of a university trash-free. When his department wanted to use temporary help, the full-time workers were forced out. He was very proud of his work record and his ability to maintain a job.

After dating for about three months, we began looking at mobile homes. Since Wayne was already retired, we wanted something that could be paid for by the time I retired. When we were discussing signing the loan, Wayne had not yet officially popped the question.

So one day I asked him, "Are we going to get married?"

"Well, we know we will."

"How do you know for sure if you haven't even asked me?"

Finally, he was persuaded to ask, and I told him, "Yes."

We laughed about that many times. Two months later, we had a simple church wedding with family and close friends.

Wayne was cheerful and fun and loved to laugh. We often had friends for dinner. Wayne learned to do most of the cleaning for an event, while I worked on the cooking. We made a good pair. We were involved in church, made some good friends, and did everything together. I liked to play pranks on him, such as hiding all his coffee cups or turning his big chair upside down. The dog was always blamed. He took it all in good humor.

My sense of fun and laughter was a saving point for me. When I was young, my family received a farming magazine with a joke page. I'd read these jokes to my mom, who would make me stand and tell one when we had company. I absorbed the idea of acceptance through humor. This was a very valuable asset during my struggles.

Counselor's Note: The Power of Humor

In his book *The Five Love Languages*, author Gary Chapman describes the major ways that people give and receive love. Acts of service, gifts, quality time, physical touch, and words of affirmation are fundamental languages in which to connect and share one's deepest affections for another. Humor is another vital avenue for connection and intimacy with others. Watch any couple in love and you will see them tickling, teasing, and giggling at inside secrets. Babies coo and giggle before they can even talk. For trauma victims, healing and connection with others may more easily occur in an environment balanced with comfort, nurture, and laughter.

Even though I didn't know how to give or receive love, Wayne and I were good to each other and for each other. He did his best to show me he loved me, and there were moments when I almost believed it, but because I never opened myself to him or told him anything about my past, I always had the suspicion that his love included only what he could see. I thought that if he ever learned who the real me was, he'd be gone. I did not give him my heart; I did not know how and did not even realize my lack. In a way, I did love him, using the only course of action I understood: doing for him. I thought that was the way to love and please.

We enjoyed each other for seven and a half years. Then early one Sunday morning he got up and fell; he had had a stroke. After being in ICU for three days, he had another stroke. He was on life support, but now he was brain dead, so the support was removed, and in a few minutes, he passed away.

A Wave of Grace

God's grace continued:

- *Wayne and I met.*
- *We had seven and a half happy years together.*
- *Wayne and I were best friends and helped each other.*
- *Wayne was a fine Christian man with good morals: no smoking, drinking, foul language, indecent magazines or movies, or out-of-control temper. He was cheerful and outgoing, thoughtful and kind, one of the best blessings of my life.*

4

Tom
(Age Sixty-Three to Sixty-Six)

Cracking the Window

Wayne died just three weeks before the beginning of a new school year. I had been teaching for almost thirty years, but, as can be imagined, I had great difficulty that year. I did not begin well and gradually sank lower and lower, until a friend and fellow teacher could see how I was struggling and recommended a Christian counselor she knew. I didn't like the idea of seeing a male counselor, since I didn't like the male population very much, but Tom [his name has been changed] was definitely sent by God.

It was not easy to sit in a counselor's office. Talking about any topic except the most mundane was always difficult, as it is for many people. God knew what He was doing when He sent me to Tom. Tom was easygoing, not abrupt or demanding, and yet he could draw an answer from me. True, sometimes there were long pauses, but eventually I was able to answer.

Four topics were discussed consistently in our sessions: boundaries, relationships, identity, and grace.

B—What are boundaries?

R—I had no close relationship with anyone.

I—Identity? Who or what am I?

G—I had no clue about grace.

The interesting acrostic spelled with the four terms is *brig,* exactly where the lack of knowledge in these areas had imprisoned me for nearly sixty years!

A Constant Companion

The thought of suicide had been a daily occurrence since my first attempt at nineteen or twenty and for most of the next forty years. At times, the desire would subside, but usually it was a constant companion. Many times every day, I thought, *It doesn't matter; I won't be here long anyway.* I had a very definite plan, which was not likely to fail as the other two attempts had. Tom wanted to institutionalize me, but I had had enough of that in prior years. To avoid that possibility, at the end of each session, he would have me promise that I would be back the next week. I never could lie to Tom, so when I promised him, I would do it. Actually, I always thought that sometime he would forget to ask, and I would have a chance to act, but he never did neglect to make me promise. It was worth not being committed to a hospital again.

When people talked, it was often meaningless jabber to me. They could just as well be reciting *"Rub-a-dub-dub"* for all it meant. I could hear the words, could repeat them back, in fact, but the words had no meaning. It was like the imaginary radio I heard playing a lot. Even though the radio wasn't real, I could hear it in the distance, a news talk show with different voices speaking, but I could never quite distinguish what was being said—almost, but not quite. It was the same way when someone talked to me; I could hear the words but couldn't distinguish what they meant.

One Thursday, I asked Tom, "Why do I believe the negative comments from a few parents, when I know what they say isn't true?"

"You always took the blame, even for your early abuse when you were only six."

"Well, then, why won't I accept the compliments that many more give me?"

"You don't believe people are telling the truth, and the encouraging words just bounce off your protective armor. You don't feel as if you deserve anything good," Tom replied.

"Is that why I give so much of my stuff away? I'll buy something I want, and then I'll give it to the next person who comes along. I've given away a lot of even expensive things."

"Yes. You feel you are too bad and don't deserve to enjoy anything. You are trying to buy friendship, because you think no one likes you just for who you are."

"I don't see how anybody could."

"I do."

How could I respond to that?

> *Journal, July 11, 2009*
> *What a horrible dream I had! I was riding on a carousel which was spinning so fast that my head was pulled outside of the edge. All around, right up to the edge, were hurtful objects—knives, rocks, briars. When her head would sling out it would hit these objects. Evil people held those things and when she hit, they would laugh a hideous laugh. They were making jokes as she was dying little by little.*

After six months with Tom, I began to see glimpses of a better life that might be possible for me. Sometimes I would think I had really gained some understanding of a spiritual concept, such as forgiveness or mercy, but I had trouble holding the ideas in my head. They would slip out, and I would need to cover the same ground again and again. Tom was very patient.

We often discussed the problems I had building friendships. During one counseling session, I told Tom, "This weekend I helped some friends move."

"Did you want to do that?"

"Not really."

"Then why did you?"

"They needed my truck, and I didn't trust them to just take it."

"Do you visit them very often?"

I shook my head. "I don't visit them. I just know them from church."

"But you can work for them?"

"That's what I did." I shrugged.

"How would you feel if you just sat down and visited with these friends you helped move?"

I sighed. "I'd rather work."

"Is this the way it is with God, too?"

"Yeah." I paused. "Yeah."

"Here's your homework assignment for the week. I'd like you to journal about this topic: 'If, for one hour, I visited with the people I helped move, what would I talk about, and how would I feel?'"

I did the journaling as Tom suggested. It was helpful because it was very specific. Generalities were not beneficial for me, because I could not understand how to apply them in various situations. When I was instructed exactly what to do in a particular circumstance, I learned. Only when I became more skillful in relationships, was I able to employ general suggestions.

> *Journal, August 18, 2009*
> *A lot of pressure has lightened. I used to feel physically pressed down all the time and felt such pressure from everywhere. The constant turmoil has lessened some, too. I still am very uncomfortable with myself, though, as if the pieces don't fit and the puzzle doesn't make a picture.*

About this time, I took the Living Bible to read a favorite passage, one that I had tried to believe for a long time: Ephesians 1:4–6. It spoke!

1. God chose us! It didn't have anything to do with our performance, because He decided to do this, not only before we were born but way back before the world was even created.

2. God made another decision: to make us holy and faultless. It's not as if He didn't know what we would be like, but He decided that was the way He would see us, not necessarily "holy" but "holy in His eyes."

3. God's third decision has always been to adopt us. Again, since it had been decided long ago, it has nothing to do with our actions, words, or thoughts. It's similar to choosing sides for baseball, and one captain's first choice is the worst player because that kid is his best friend. God chose us just because He likes us!

To have understood, however briefly it was, that God chose me, made me holy, and adopted me was definitely His grace at work. Even if I lost the thought, I touched it, and it would return. In fact, most insights that I had began briefly and disappeared, only to resurface later. This usually happened many times before I fully comprehended.

My opinion of God began to alter. I would have moments when I believed what the Bible stated about Him. My mindset, though, often twisted the words into something quite different. As the fear and shame lessened, the times of clarity became more frequent. My confidence in God grew and became stronger. The following poem was written, after I had been working with Tom for a few months, during one of my first moments of trust:

God Understands
The cries, those made with silent sobs;
The tears, those checked which never fall;
The aches and pains, the weariness;
God understands—He knows it all.
The sighs, those silence keep encased;
The mounts, which leave man feeling small;
The cares and hurts, the burdened hearts;
God understands—He lifts it all.
The wounds, which one can never share;
The blows which shock, dismay, appall;
The fires and floods, the gnawing griefs;
God understands—He loves us all.
All anguish of the human soul
That would beset or work to fall;
God understands—He's watching o'er;
He knows and lifts and loves us all.

> *Journal, August 15, 2009*
> *I am making progress, although I cannot think of a single specific right now. Oh, yes, I can! I'm generally happier; I'm more alert and interested in doing something; I enjoy my teaching more; I laugh more easily and tell more jokes; I play with the dogs more.*

The many books on grace that I had read, reread, and studied so much could be summarized with one statement: who I am is not based on what I do or have done, good or bad, but on what Jesus has done. That statement overturned a lot of former misconceptions regarding how I thought and felt as I did about myself and others. I was not weird or demonic; I was living with the natural results of my experiences. Best of all, there was hope for change, and Tom said he would help. Hope and help were all I needed. A little light had switched on.

I thanked Tom for all his hard work, for encouraging me and believing in me. Sometimes I even thought that he cared if I lived or died, although I didn't know why. *He can just get another client,* I thought.

Feelings Are Trouble

Therapy brought up things I had not thought of for a while. Old feelings and old fears reappeared. My dad's sexual abuse was fondling, not rape, but I feared rape from him for many of my young years. As this journal entry reveals, the old emotion was still present:

> Journal, August 22, 2009
> Last night I dreamed about my dad again. I was a teen
> and did something he didn't like. He threatened me with
> the question, "Do you want me to rape you?"

I hated being female. All my life it had been an open sore. I mentioned this half a dozen times to Tom but never would pursue it. Males had power and were dangerous. Females were always vulnerable. No matter how influential they were, or what high position they had, females could always be raped. There was no way a female could escape that constant danger; it was always present. It was safer not to be too open or friendly with others. Stay distant and closed. Rapes usually occurred with acquaintances, not strangers, so if I were a stranger to everyone, the chance of rape would be less.

It was becoming clear how my thinking and responding had been based on childhood experiences. I never could understand that before, couldn't see the connection, but now I was beginning to. So how could I remove the hold of the past? How could I get rid of my chains?

Every area I had problems with seemed to boil down to one factor: I was not worthy. I was not worthy to have a nice home or pretty clothes, to receive compliments, to accept what God says and wants to give, to believe people care for me, etc. My cruelty to myself only let up after five years of intensive therapy.

Journaling, too, aggravated memories from long ago. Many times, as I was writing about one problem, another related issue would pop up. Some people have said things they didn't know until the words came out of their mouth. That's the way writing was for me. Quite often, when I would be journaling, I'd write something I didn't really know until the words appeared. Writing about feelings was easier for me than talking about them. The following journal entry communicates the distress I was experiencing:

> *Journal, September 16, 2009*
> *When all the abuse happened to me, it's as if I died inside. When I was dead, how could I have any feelings? Why would anything matter anymore? To be dead is not to feel or care. I put my mind in neutral and became blank. What would I do if I actually felt all the feelings that came? What would happen to me? It is a relief to be a nonperson. Then it no longer matters what is done to me; I'm just an object.*
>
> *At the time, the family abuse was hated but was tolerated by me. I was a child; I didn't know anything different. After all, the Lord's Prayer was prayed before meals, my dad read a chapter of the Bible out loud after supper, and I went to church and sat next to my brothers. It must have been okay.*
>
> *Oh, I wish I could cry. It has been twenty-five years or more since the first year of Bible school, when I would cry every night, so torn over the life I was living. Then I never cried anymore after that.*

When I told Tom I was beginning to feel like a person, he asked me how that felt. I thought about that question for several weeks. Here are a few specifics:

- Everything looks brighter, as if I left a dark room and stepped into the sunshine.
- I have preferences and favorites. I had never had a favorite food, color, restaurant, or anything else.
- I have more connection with people instead of total isolation.
- Sometimes I feel equal with others.
- It matters when things happen to me.
- I'm included in God's promises.
- I can recognize myself in a mirror and in glass doors as I walk past.
- I don't feel overpowered all the time.
- Sometimes I don't feel dirty or unclean.
- I don't get as frustrated with myself.
- I recognize my name immediately.
- I don't bang my head at all anymore.
- I know where I am when I'm driving.
- I don't think all people are dangerous.
- Some days I do more than cope.
- Sometimes I can ask for help.

Counselor's Note: Small Steps

Often people in therapy or early recovery from abuse measure their success by how often they think about the abuse, their feelings and mood, or the number of distressing symptoms they still experience. Nancy measured her progress in small, tangible steps. This patient, insightful approach to recovery not only prevented her from quitting therapy prematurely, but it also allowed her to celebrate her small successes and continue with the long, uphill journey to recovery.

One day, after I had been working with Tom for a year and a half, I entered his office very discouraged.

"What's happening?" he asked.

"The same old stuff that just keeps coming up and coming up."

"It takes time. You have a lot of years to sift through."

"That's just it! I *don't* get through."

"I think you are making very good progress. Can you see places where you've grown?"

"The same junk keeps stewing inside. The past is who I am." I was frustrated and discouraged with my seeming lack of progress.

"Yes, the past is part of who you are, but only part, and furthermore, it does not dictate the future. Some of the things you've been involved with bother you, but you haven't touched these past activities for many years. The only parts in the present are your memories and feelings."

"I don't do much about that either."

"I'll help you until you get it." Wonderful words to hear!

One day I drove thirty miles away and dumped all three dogs and the cat on the side of a dirt road. It wasn't that I didn't want them anymore, but they were too good to be around me. I didn't deserve them.

Two days later a storm came up, and I thought about the dogs out in the thunder and lightning. They were so afraid of storms and rain. Immediately I grabbed their food and water and went to look for them. I prayed to find them but didn't make any deals with God. I knew I didn't deserve a good answer, but they deserved one. When I drove to where I had dumped them and began calling, in just two or three minutes the three dogs, but no cat, came dashing out of the woods. I really didn't expect that to happen. If they had stayed by the road, I thought they'd be run over, but if they had gone very far into the woods, I thought they'd be lost. They climbed right into the truck, wagging their tails and licking my face. Why is God so good to me? It was ridiculous to try to get rid of the cat and dogs. After all, when I was gone, somebody would take them anyway. I didn't have to do anything with them then. I wasn't thinking right.

During the storm, the dogs were on my lap, very frightened and shaking. I was petting them and talking to them, and was so glad they were with me and not out in the rain somewhere. It was easy to see the correlation between the dogs with their fear and me with my fear. Several times during the loud thunder, Maggie jerked up as if to jump off my lap, and then lay back down as if she thought, *Where would I go?*

I asked out loud, "God, is there something You want me to know?"

The thought immediately came—*I'll hold You in your storms, too.*

I told the dogs that it would soon pass. Then I thought that maybe my storm would also. Perhaps I needed to wait it out like the dogs did, snuggle up to someone, and trust my Owner.

Although I've retreated to my little imaginary brick building for nearly forty years, I no longer want to live there for the rest of my life. I always thought of the building as my safety and protection, but it has become my prison. It's not my salvation but my damnation. It's where Satan, not God, wants me, but when people start closing in, where could I go? It's similar to the old Western movies where the sheriff would have three or four gunmen moving in, step by step, with their hands on their holsters, getting closer and closer. I could take off and not come back, or I could never speak again. *There might be one more option,* I thought, *stuff the tailpipe and start the truck.*

> *Journal, September 12, 2010*
> *I'm thinking of suicide a lot. I might not actually even dare do it, but if I concentrate on it, take just one step at a time, I think I could. My life is not bad, but I'm tired of tending to everything. I don't want to do anything, and there's no enjoyment. I feel like an old, old person, and I don't want to be bothered anymore.*
> *It's not that I'm so anxious to kill myself. I feel so sad all the time, very sad. Sad and lost. Being sucked down into a hole. Drowning. Feels like I'm drowning. It's a deep, deep sadness, but I don't know why. And I don't know why I've had this as far back as I can remember. All I can pray is "Help me, God."*

Tom told me I needed to tell someone if I intended to attempt suicide. Even if I couldn't say the words, I needed to express it some way. It would be a very final decision, possibly my last. I was not sure that that was how I would want to be remembered. Neither was I positive I would even be remembered. Immediately, I realized that was not true. I had some friends who loved me. Why was that so hard to say and accept? I never noticed that I looked away when someone complimented me or said she loved me until my supervisor told me. It was harder to look in the eye of someone who praised me than someone who found fault with me.

I was beginning to have some emotions but was having trouble keeping a balance between having no emotions and running my life by them. Most of my years, I had rejected or negated them, but at that time it seemed as if I sometimes ran my life by them. The days I didn't feel like taking a shower, I didn't. Many Sundays I didn't go to church. I canceled doctor appointments, didn't call people I needed to, didn't talk much. I didn't do what I didn't want to do. I went to work, though, and brushed my teeth and fed the dogs and saw Tom. That was about all.

After twenty years of no alcohol, I began to drink again. The rising of emotions was very stressful, and drinking was a familiar method of relieving stress. Every day after work, as soon as I set foot in the house, I would pour my first vodka and would keep on drinking until I fell into bed.

Tom often assigned homework for me to complete before our next session. When I began serious work on feelings, he thought the senses were a good place to start. He would have me pay attention to my surroundings for five minutes and list everything my five senses told me. I did this many times in a variety of places.

One unusual assignment Tom gave was to make eye contact with someone for five seconds. I seldom looked at anyone directly for even one second. He went to the computer to print out a reminder for me.

"How long did I say?"

"Two seconds."

He laughed and said, "It was five, but since you said two, I'll make it ten seconds."

I laughed, too, but it was a long time before I was able to do that assignment.

Counselor's Note: Sensory Awareness

According to Dr. Bruce Perry, author of *The Boy Who Was Raised as a Dog*, those who have experienced sexual abuse have varying levels of sensory awareness. Those people whose bodies reacted to the abuse with a "fight" response induced by the brain's natural stimulants might have a hypersensitive awareness to the environment around them. Others, like Nancy, whose bodies reacted to the abuse by "flight or freeze," responding by detaching or disassociating, have a reduced sense of the world around them. By becoming attuned to the sights, sounds, and feel of her external environment, Nancy's body and brain could begin the arduous process of befriending her once-dangerous world.

I Am a Person

I also read many helpful books, brought them to counseling, and discussed my comments and questions with Tom. He loaned me the book *Boundaries* by Cloud and Townsend. I remember how incomprehensible this book was and told Tom that I had read the first hundred pages three times and had no idea what it was talking about. He advised me to continue through the book, and then we would discuss it. We did, and I began to understand an entirely new concept of what personal space and boundaries mean. This type of reading and learning happened many times and was so very helpful to me.

I thought I might not make it through the year, through the Christmas season. I tried to think what would make me happy, what would bring me joy. Activities with friends were beginning to be helpful, and working with Tom helped, but I felt I was too dependent on him. It seemed dangerous. And the writing seemed stupid, saying the exact same words for the umpteenth time.

Even with all the times of being down, I realized that after two years of professional Christian counseling, I was beginning to view God differently. I was responding in new ways, and was even considering the possibility that I was a person—all very amazing to me. What was so mind-boggling was the fact that all I did was talk about my life and thoughts; I was not really trying to force a change at all, yet the changes were occurring. How could this just happen? It was and still is a puzzle to me. So I did not stop working with Tom.

———~~~०००ഌᎧᎧᎧᎧᲔᎧᎧ०००~~~———

A Wave of Grace

Now I know and believe Psalm 139:17, "How precious also are thy thoughts unto me, O God!" Tom was the first person I had trusted since my grandparents passed away when I was twelve. That opened my heart's door a little, and I tentatively began two or three other relationships. Their response was so loving that I began to trust God a bit. That opened the door further—to trust others more, then God more, etc. An upward spiral began that is still expanding today.

———~~~०००ഌᎧᎧᎧᎧᲔᎧᎧ०००~~~———

Hope began to appear now and then, gradually, then more frequently and for longer periods. This was inconsistent, though, and sometimes I could drop down for several weeks. Slowly the low times became shorter and not as deep. There were times that I didn't ever want to talk or smile again. On the other hand, I often felt free to enjoy doing whatever I was doing at the time, be it planting flowers, cleaning the house, or playing a board game with a friend.

Socializing was difficult. Getting close to someone could be downright dangerous. I would arrange to do something or have someone visit, but when the time came closer, I would be irritated that I had made those plans and often cancelled with some excuse. The idea of being with someone seemed fine when the thought arose, but I usually changed my mind. This, too, ever so slowly was modified by discussing it repeatedly with Tom. Overall, both my personal life and social life had improved greatly. I explained my view of my life at that time to a friend: "I have a lot of ups and downs, it's true, but I used to have only downs; now at least I have some ups, too."

For a few years, I had wanted to feel love for others. I did things for people but didn't feel anything, so it didn't seem real. Slowly I began to think a bit differently about it. A lack of feelings did not mean a lack of love. Most of the time, I helped because the person needed it or wanted it. Love for God is shown by obedience, according to John 14; feelings are not even mentioned. I concluded that when I helped people who needed help, I did love them. I offered love with deeds more often than with words.

Praying to put God in His rightful place on the throne was one thing, living it was another and not so easy. I was discovering how powerful and obstinate I really was, not weak and frail as I had thought. My ego was very strong; it always wanted to be in control and on the throne that belonged to God. I began praying more than "God, forgive me" and "God, help me." I longed to be closer to Him and to possess some qualities of His.

Changes in my beliefs and feelings took place slowly. Many times, I would experience an old feeling from years ago. The current situation would be very different, but to my emotional memory, it was similar enough to evoke an identical response. The following journal entry is an example:

> *Journal, March 15, 2011*
> *While talking in counseling today, Tom asked about how I felt and if I was lonely. I said that I couldn't depend on anyone. An old feeling became so vivid that I couldn't speak for several minutes. Then I said that life was dangerous, and I needed to pull back. Years ago, I never knew what would happen. Life was unsettled, and I didn't know what would come next. I could not control my world. To escape physically was not possible, so I kept busy or drank or hid and tried not to think. Sometimes I still feel that way: out of control, all alone, helpless, afraid.*

Counselor's Note: Triggers and Emotional Memory

When a trauma survivor encounters a present-day experience that resembles a past experience, often emotions from that past abuse will surface in the present. These experiences are called triggers, and may take the form of a sight, smell, sound, touch, or word. Triggers activate what's called an emotional memory. When an event or experience is perceived by the brain to have vital importance to our survival, the brain will code the memory with powerful emotions so that, when we encounter a similar experience in the future, we will have the added benefit of the powerful emotion to activate our limbic system.

Apparently, the word "lonely" was a trigger that evoked a powerful emotional memory in Nancy. She wrote in her journal that she felt the world was dangerous and that she needed to "pull back." This flight response is fitting for someone who remembers at an emotional level being isolated, alone, and afraid.

A Wave of Grace

Realistically, though, life no longer seems unsettled or dangerous. Neither do I need addictions to cope. I am in control and living intentionally. I have some good friends, too, and the best Friend of all. This friend and Savior gives me the strength and ability to live for Him (Isaiah 41:10 and 13). His presence in me provides the peace (Philippians 4:7) and security I need to socialize with people.

<u>Signs of Healing</u>

I am not where I want to be or where I am going to be, but I definitely am not where I used to be either. My thinking has changed in a multitude of areas:

- I'm a person, a real person.
- I don't really need the little brick building anymore.
- I'm not at fault for abuse done to me.
- There are some things I enjoy and enjoy doing.
- My memory has improved.
- I don't feel as if I'm a fake all the time.
- I don't feel inferior to my students.
- I am trusting God a lot more, even some people a little.
- I can recognize anger in myself, and sometimes it is okay.
- I often give myself a little leeway.
- I am better at making decisions I want instead of what others want.
- I don't always jump all over myself when I make a mistake.
- I am getting into my spirit that God loves me.
- I am gaining assurance of forgiveness and heaven.
- I can pray and believe God is caring.
- I think there are several people who care about me.
- I can make decisions about what is important for me.
- Guilt is not constantly hanging over me.

A Wave of Grace
The list is incredible, even several years later—almost as if
it referred to someone else. To know it refers to me gives me
a mountain of gratitude to God and His goodness.

Tom's listening skill and wise words were affecting my faulty thinking. I knew that the way I processed information and relationships was not beneficial to me. I was willing to change. The following poem shows how my thinking had shifted:

Then Jesus Comes
When life seems hopeless, just about to fold,
And all the daily problems press and push you,
The future's dark, and weary is the road—
Then Jesus comes and gives you life anew.
When all the past is blotched, the pages torn,
And there's no way to go that's right for you,
When you look back with shame, can't help but mourn—
Then Jesus comes and gives you life anew.

Since I was so deficient in the feelings area, I thought about it a lot. Feelings were important to help me figure out what was happening so I could deal with it and move forward. I had spent two years trying to understand this, and I could see why it took so long. The topic was very complex. When I first began with Tom, I didn't have any feelings, and when I began to realize that I did, I couldn't identify them. When I learned to identify how I felt, I didn't know why I was feeling that way and would get angry with myself. Later, I could sometimes determine the reason. Feelings could help me decide what to do in a situation, and the acknowledgment of it prevented me from burying that feeling. This might be so obvious to most people, but it was a brand new idea for me. A lot of time and effort had been put on this process, but it was worth every bit. The ability to begin distinguishing feelings was a big factor in helping me feel as a person.

Tom said that I was beginning to notice some positives about myself and should make a list. This was much harder than thinking of the negatives and took quite some time to do, but I did manage to write a few:

- I root for the underdog.
- I can see things that need to be done.
- I am handy with simple tools and jobs.

- I see the funny side of things.
- I see details.
- I like to help.
- I am able to see correlations.
- I can tell a joke well.
- I have some emotions.

A Wave of Grace

To actually see some good things about myself, all I can say is Wow! It took over two years with Tom, but what a great gift to myself! It's a good feeling.

Counselor's Note: Antidote to Shame

Shame is often the most painful and enduring experience one struggles with after trauma and abuse. Children who have been abused often believe the abuse was their fault and that they are bad and disgusting. Shame becomes a near-permanent reality in their minds, and decisions made during their teen and young adult years often emerge out of a need to escape or a need to transfer the shame to someone else.

When shame is neutralized by the nurturing acceptance of others, the victimized child or adult may eventually internalize love, just as she once internalized shame. This response to love takes time and repeated experiences with grace and forgiveness in order to become the child's new identity and approach to self.

Grace has been a difficult topic for me to understand. I've studied many Bible verses and read several books about grace trying to comprehend the love and work of God in a person's life. When I spend several hours a week reading this kind of book, I do better emotionally.

In the spring of 2011, I deliberately began searching for God's grace in the story of my life. I was surprised to find it so evident in every part. Here is the list I made at that time:

- By His grace, I survived two suicide attempts.
- By His grace, I've been teaching at a wonderful school for thirty-one years.
- By His grace, I have good friends.
- By His grace, Tom is my counselor.
- By His grace, my house is paid for.
- By His grace, I'm saved and sure of it.
- By His grace, I've always been interested in spiritual things.
- By His grace, hope is rising in me.
- By His grace, I have a wonderful class with very supportive parents.
- By His grace, my dogs like to snuggle.
- By His grace, my viewpoint of God has changed.
- By His grace, my health is excellent.
- By His grace, my church preaches the Word.
- By His grace, the love of God is being made real in my heart.

Often, on the way home from counseling, I would talk to myself. Sometimes I felt or thought I was not doing very well. In actuality, though, my worst days were better than my best days used to be. I needed to give myself as much leeway as I gave to others. When I was discussing my thoughts on this subject with Tom, he gave me the wonderful illustration of reconstructive surgery.

Some burn cases could have forty or fifty surgeries, and they still probably didn't look like everyone else, but they continued until they got to the best that they could be. This was exactly what had been happening to me with the restructuring of so much of who I was. Sometimes I thought that Tom must wonder if I was ever going to get with the program, but he never gave any hint of that. He was only caring, kind, and patient. He, of all people, should have known how long something like this would take. It would be faster and easier to work from the outside in, but it would not be true healing. This is similar to repairing a wobbly chair: the pieces must be pulled apart and glued from the inside or the repair won't hold.

———∿∿◦◖❍◗◦❍❦❍◗◦◦∿∿———

A Wave of Grace
Thank the good Lord for all the reconstructive surgery He
has done, what He is continuing to do, and all He will still
do in the future. God is rebuilding me from the inside out.

———∿∿◦◖❍◗◦❍❦❍◗◦◦∿∿———

Who Am I?

I wanted to improve, and I worked diligently. Similar to dieting, there were weak moments, weak days, yes, and weak weeks. I hated that I was human. That sounds funny to me, but it was true. I needed to be patient with myself. The legalistic church I attended for my first seventeen years still had a hold on me, but its grip had weakened a lot. I thought of two good things about being human: Jesus was born of a human and died for humans.

Technically, I wasn't socially stupid; I was socially inept. I think social graces are usually caught and little taught, but with all that was happening when I was a child, I probably wasn't attuned to what should have been caught. In our chaotic house, probably not as much was taught as needed to be either. In addition, after the abuse began, I was too occupied with survival to pay much attention to anything else. I lived with that lack of knowledge on a daily basis.

Tom helped me with many situations. Usually I didn't even notice the social graces people displayed; it all went over my head. For example, after school was dismissed, the other fourth-grade teachers would get together and visit until the last few students were picked up. Even standing with them and listening, I couldn't figure out what they were talking about. I didn't seem to be able to understand. Tom asked me if one of these teachers could give me a clue in this situation, so I explained my dilemma to Shannon. For the remainder of the school year, when I approached the group, Shannon would speak to me and say that so-and-so was talking about such-and-such. That was all it took and was a tremendous help. The following year, I was able to do this on my own.

In social settings, the usual way I managed was to say something funny, and that generally got me through. A dozen times a day, I didn't know how to respond. If it seemed I was put on the spot, even a little, I immediately felt pressured and couldn't think of a response. It helped to anticipate what would be said, but I was not savvy enough to do that very often. It was this way with most adults. I didn't have the problem with children. That was one reason why counseling was so difficult, especially at first. I said "It doesn't matter" so often to Tom that one day he drew a circle, wrote "It doesn't matter" in the center, and then placed a diagonal line through it. No longer was I allowed to say those words. Although I wanted the help, it was hard to answer the questions and talk. Often I didn't know or couldn't explain how I felt. I had been an escape artist all my life, but somehow I got enough grit to stay on the path that God had laid out for me.

Counselor's Note: Social Intelligence

In his book, *Social Intelligence*, author and researcher Daniel Goleman describes social intelligence as the ability to tune into one's social world, to understand that world, and to respond appropriately to the social cues and needs of others. The foundation of social intelligence is built on early experiences in one's own family. If that foundation is laced with dangerous and shaming experiences, then that child may not continue to tune into and mimic healthy social interactions. Furthermore, the traumatized child in a chronic disassociated state will lack the focus needed to learn adequately how to relate to and understand others.

During her recovery, Nancy absorbed enough of the nurturing acceptance from her friends and counselor to begin to tune in to her social world, thus kick-starting her dormant social brain.

—⁓⊶⊙⊶⊙⊷⊙⊶⊙⊷⊙⊷⊙⊶⁓—

A Wave of Grace

I have improved in social skills. I am beginning to care for a few people who don't make demands on me and who seem to like me just as I am without any particular performance. It's still hard for me to read people, but I am finding it easier to approach others to just listen or join in. The social insight that I am gaining is amazing to me. I haven't much of a start, but it is a start, and I am excited.

—⁓⊶⊙⊶⊙⊷⊙⊶⊙⊷⊙⊷⊙⊶⁓—

I had taught thirty-one years at the same Christian school. Parents and other teachers seemed to respect me. Apparently, they didn't see me the same way I did. My supervisor told me frequently that I was a master teacher, an exceptionally good master teacher. I didn't know how that was possible.

God has been good to me. Probably the best thing He has done, other than giving His Son, was to give me friends throughout my lifetime. He did this so I would have life and joy. They did not turn against me; I was the one who so often ignored them and let them go. Satan wanted to destroy me by isolating me. He knew that I didn't have much chance on my own. Probably no one would. We were made to be sociable. The social arena was a great area for the devil to work; he usually got good results. That fact told me I needed to make this a much higher priority. When I was outgoing, I felt as if I were faking, but as I became used to companionship, it felt more real. I intended to go slowly, but I was ready to be a better friend.

———∿∿∙ᎧᏋᏓᏬᏋᎧᏕ∙∿∿———

A Wave of Grace

Sometimes I get a bit disheartened, thinking I'm not making much progress, but usually I am extremely encouraged, almost dancing with joy over who I am becoming. The second part is a lot stronger than it used to be. The first part pops up occasionally but doesn't stay for long. Encouragement, so valuable to my soul, is pushing into my very being. That is exactly what keeps me moving forward.

———∿∿∙ᎧᏋᏓᏬᏋᎧᏕ∙∿∿———

I finally learned that I was more than the sum of my experiences. When God was put into the equation, and God was always in, an entirely different answer was computed. As a child, I was prayed for by my maternal grandparents, and at twelve when I turned to Jesus, I had the Holy Spirit to help and guide me. Even during those grievous years in Minnesota, I had never rejected Jesus. Though often without hope, I knew He was my only Hope. I knew if I were ever to understand life, it would be through my relationship with God.

God's holiness has always frightened me. Look at Cain: one sin and God rejected him. Look at Saul: one disobedient act and he was out! My list was long, but I was learning to look at someone else, the One who took all my sins on Himself and paid the price for me to be redeemed and free. His redemption didn't depend on how little sin I had done, although it wasn't *little*, or how much good I had done, although it wasn't *much*. It wasn't about me at all. I did not get heart understanding until recently. I knew it in my head, and I taught it, but until the blinders that Satan affixed on me as a child were removed, I had no heart belief.

Changes

Bit by bit, Tom presented biblical principles concerning who I was. After a while, cracks appeared in my self-righteousness, for I began to consider that my self-sufficiency might be the basic problem. My experiences taught me not to depend on anyone else, not even God, and although in some ways I hated myself, actually I was lifting myself up to the status of a god. When I believed my opinion more than I believed what God said, I was making myself superior to Him. That revelation was a hard pill to swallow but essential for permanent change to occur. When Jesus called Lazarus out of the tomb, Lazarus was still totally bound by grave clothes from head to foot. Instead of speaking them gone, Jesus told the bystanders to "loose him and let him go" (John 11:44). Ordinary people did this for him, and God is using others to remove my shackles, too.

A Wave of Grace

When I finally let God be God, more good changes happened. I saw that there were people who loved me and who, in turn, made God's love more real. As God's love became a reality, I noticed more love from people. Even with frequent downs, I am now experiencing an upward spiral. I have a heart grasp of God's grace and forgiveness, and I can see His main plan for me is to be not to do. And what I actually do flows out of who I am in Him. It's not the same as my thinking of ways to work for Him.

Recovering from sexual abuse, especially after a lifetime of living out of that mindset, was a long haul. I did not know it would take so long, but I was thrilled about my emerging life and certainly was not going to quit counseling. Often, when another layer peeled off, it was too much to handle. Either I wanted to just sit and do nothing, or I worked myself to a frazzle. Progress was as up and down as a mountain trail, but when I stopped long enough to look, I could see how far I had climbed.

I began to see myself as a person now. When I sat and saw my legs extended, I knew they were mine. When I drank a cup of coffee, I knew my hands were bringing the cup to my lips. Although it used to be a relief not to be involved in what was happening around me, I started to live in the present and enjoy it.

The imaginary brick building in which I had hidden for so long was gone. It gradually disappeared, and God became my refuge. I trusted Him more and more. I could pray about my concerns and knew that God heard me, loved me, and would do what was best for me.

For months, I studied Romans 5–8 and wrote a notebook full of comments and questions over these chapters. This diligent search made a huge difference in my view of God. Later, I realized this study was the Holy Spirit shoveling out the long-held concepts (dead ashes) and shoveling in the new (live coals) to bring in light and warmth.

Then I began working through Galatians. I identified with the people of Galatia who believed in grace for salvation and in works to live the Christian life. Much freedom came when I understood that Jesus left nothing out, that there was nothing to do and nothing to add. Galatians 2:16 taught me that I only needed faith in Jesus Christ.

A Wave of Grace
To know there is no requirement for salvation, that it is by
faith alone, was a tremendous revelation. And I believed it!

Although a lack of interpersonal skills continued to plague me, even after three years of working with Tom, I could see a little light. I realized that the word *social* implies that they are passed from person to person. That meant that I could still pick up some of these skills by listening to and observing others. Actually, I could see that I had already done a lot of that. My awareness of others was improving. Occasionally, I was able to figure out ahead of time how someone might respond. I was farther down the road than I had been. I still had many miles to go, but I didn't feel as awkward as I previously had in many social situations.

Boiling Pot of Anger

During much of the third year with Tom, we worked on feelings, especially anger in the last few months. With my experiences, I understood why I could have anger issues, but I had never expressed it and didn't think I had any. At that time, though, my anger began surfacing. Soon it was boiling over but only at therapy. I was so afraid of being angry and losing control that I didn't bring it up anywhere else. After sessions of expressing my anger, I hated myself. I didn't know how to handle all of this; it was overwhelming. One time, in the middle of a session, I told Tom that I was tired of this and was just going to disappear.

"Are you thinking about suicide?" he asked.

"I don't know what I'm thinking."

"Do you have a plan?"

"Yes," I admitted.

"What is it?"

"Stuff the tailpipe."

"You know, I'll have to do something about that."

"Just do whatever you want!" I stomped out, very angry, and drove home.

Thirty minutes later a policeman was at my door. He asked how I was doing and if I was okay. He said Tom had called saying I might kill myself and asked, "Is that true?" I denied everything because I was afraid I would be committed to the psychiatric ward of some hospital. The officer was very kind, handed me his card, and said he was on duty all night and for me to call anytime; he would be glad to come and talk. This entire incident scared me. Even though I did not want to return to Tom, the desire to get well was stronger. I tried not to show my anger again in his office, but I knew I still had a reservoir.

Counselor's Note: What to Expect in Early Recovery

In their book, *The Courage to Heal*, authors Ellen Bass and Laura Davis describe the thirteen stages of healing from sexual abuse. The second stage, called the Emergency Stage, often occurs after someone decides to address past abuse. Women may experience deep depression, feelings of helplessness, confusion, and suicidal obsessions. This stage comes as a shock, especially after the initial relief of disclosing the abuse. Women in this stage need the encouragement and support from close friends and counselors, as the panic and pain will eventually subside.

In December of the third year, I began having nightmares again. Although the majority of my dreams had always been nightmares, they had begun to lessen. Now they worsened, and I was dreaming night after night about getting raped. Tom knew I was getting down to the core abuse issues, and that I was now ready to delve into the trauma at a much deeper level. He explained that he was not experienced enough to process this with me the way I needed it done. I could either keep him as my counselor, and he would read and talk with other experienced therapists to get informed enough to help me, or he would give me a list of trauma counselors, and I could transfer to one of them. Since this was shortly after the police incident, and I thought he was retaliating, I was very rude and sarcastic to him. When he made me understand the real issue, I calmed down and chose to transfer. I regretted my crude attitude of the previous few months. Although I was not aware of it at that time, God was leading me to Alicia (her name has been changed).

5

Alicia
(Age Sixty-Six to Sixty-Nine)

I Meet Myself

Alicia was the exact person I needed to work with at this point. She understood everything I was dealing with and always helped me see that my actions and responses were to be expected with what I had experienced. This was a great relief to me. On the other hand, she often explained why I did not need to remain in that place. She reassured me that God was working in my life and would help me heal. As in many of the journal entries, I would often revert to third person when describing something especially painful. Alicia would stop me and ask who I was talking about, and since it was myself, would have me retell it in first person. This was hard because I was split (dissociated), but the verbal acknowledging of self certainly helped me over the next two years to come together as one person.

Right from the start, God gave me an unusual trust in Alicia, and I usually did what she suggested. When I would say, "I don't think I can do that," we would discuss it until I could. Almost immediately, I found life improving. I already had had a lot of progress the previous three years and was in much better shape beginning with her than I had been when I began with Tom. On the other hand, many tough issues were just surfacing, core issues, which I had never mentioned or even been aware of before this time.

Being with a new therapist necessitated reviewing some of the same material I had already covered with Tom. One area that I again discussed was the Bible school and what kept me there. Once again, I relived the terrible isolation of that time. "I didn't have a friend during those six years," I told Alicia, "no one to talk with, not even a dog."

All my life, I treated myself very harshly. As a child, I was never excused for my wrong behaviors. I thought of myself as evil, not as a precious and beloved daughter of God. The following journal entry portrays clearly how I thought of myself:

> *Journal, June 18, 2012*
> *While in Minnesota, I often wondered where God was. I never thought of Him being in the office with us. It would have been comforting and helpful to believe that God looked at me with love during that time, but what I believed was this: I was a Pharisee, a whitewashed sepulcher filled with dead men's bones and uncleanness (Matthew 23:27). God hates people who make the outside look good, yet the inside is full of rottenness. Would God consider my situation? I didn't think so; excuses never mattered to Him. I needed to obey—no ifs, ands, or buts. Since I was obviously living in disobedience, how could I expect His help? Hypocrites in the Bible were expected to change their ways; they couldn't expect God to bail them out. These were the only people that Jesus Himself jumped all over. How could I possibly think I was an exception?*

———— ∿⦿⦿⦿∿ ————

A Wave of Grace

Even though I was sure I did not deserve and therefore would not be offered any help from God, He did rescue me. Later, I understood the biblical definition of hypocrite. A hypocrite is someone who brags about his righteousness yet chooses to live contrary to his boast. I did not flaunt my righteousness; I always felt very sinful. Neither did I choose to live the way I did; I was compelled.

———— ∿⦿⦿⦿∿ ————

Most of the time, all thoughts about Pastor Bill had been crammed down, very compact. Now, in counseling, these dormant thoughts were pushing out of the box, greatly expanding, filling me completely. It was all I could think about. It was horrible all over again! Life was not worth living with this hanging around my neck like an albatross.

It was probably impossible to see through Pastor Bill's deception while I was in that situation. It took both being away for some time and having someone help me look at it with truth and grace. In my mind, I was filthy and worthless, reaping what I had sown.

A Wave of Grace
Sowing and reaping is a biblical principle, but this one concept is not the whole story. God's forgiveness and mercy are also biblical. God's hope and healing are biblical, as well as God's long suffering and help. And, for sure, God's grace is biblical.

Grace Group

Soon after I began work with Alicia, she received information about someone who led small groups of women survivors of childhood sexual abuse. Alicia thought I could profit from this group. It sounded scary. I was afraid the group would be too large for me to relate to. Alicia called Jane (her name has been changed), the Grace Group leader, and learned that the group maximum was six participants. That, I could manage.

Grace Group is a twelve-lesson program from Open Hearts Ministries based in Kalamazoo, Michigan. The three major divisions were as follows:

1. Telling our stories and learning to respond to others appropriately
2. Dealing with our harmful responses to the abuse
3. Learning new ways to live in victory

Some of the topics were very difficult: looking at our wounds, shame, contempt, sexuality, and brokenness. My facing these issues honestly and thoroughly has allowed the Holy Spirit to continue the healing process. The Grace Group is not intended to be a cure-all but rather a stepping-stone of understanding and healing.

At first, it was frightening, even with just six people in the group, but gradually I became accustomed to the other women and the material. We began each two-hour lesson with a short praise and prayer time and then listened to a speaker who taught the lesson and included a personal testimony. Questions regarding our life experiences were discussed. Participants were encouraged to tell their own stories, which were enlarged as the weeks continued. I didn't say much, but every week at counseling, Alicia and I reviewed the lesson and pondered the answers I had written. This helped immensely.

Counselor's Note: Support Groups

Often, when survivors of trauma come into therapy, counselors will recommend support groups in addition to individual therapy. Support groups provide additional nurture, encouragement, and education beyond the time constraints of individual therapy. Survivors need this extra boost, especially during the Emergency Stage of healing.

After a few months of working with Alicia, I began to enjoy associating with others more. Since I was able to listen better and no longer needed to plan every response, being with people was not nearly as stressful as it had been. I was learning how to observe others and learn from them. Tom and Alicia had given me many suggestions for specific situations I faced.

Seeing Alicia two times a week during the first summer I was with her helped me. When I saw her once a week, she seemed to disappear, and in my mind, she was nearly gone by the next week. This made it hard for me to begin talking. Two times a week made both sessions go well because she was completely present to me. After about six months, I didn't have that problem anymore. She was always patient and kind, easy to talk with, and full of grace, but she also presented truth every week and held that up as my goal. I knew that she cared about me.

Behind the Door of Self-Hatred

One session, while I was describing yet another dream, Alicia spoke.

"You dream so often about your brother or others trying to kill you, when all the time, you are in the process of killing yourself." She was referring to my addictive behaviors.

I nodded.

"Do you want to pray about it?"

I nodded again.

Her prayer surprised me. Alicia asked God to replace my self-hatred with His peace and asked Him to work the assurance of His love deep down in my heart. She then talked with me about the effects of my behaviors.

"God loves us, no matter what we do or don't do. But if I behave in ways that are harmful to me, there will be consequences. If I choose to smoke, and I get lung cancer, God still loves me just the same, but I will have the consequences of my behavior. Wrong choices do not negate God's love, but they do bring outcomes that may be unpleasant."

Never before had I heard cause and effect explained so clearly. I could see the truth. This discussion began a major change in my life.

After this session, my self-hatred was obvious to me as the cause of all the hurtful things I did to myself. I had not understood the results these addictions had on my life. Alicia's godly instruction helped me realize that I didn't have to do these harmful acts, but when I chose to do them, even though I didn't lose God's love, I did break fellowship with Him, and I did reinforce evil in my life. I was playing Satan's game by making myself my guide in life rather than keeping God supreme. My life didn't go very well when I took over for God.

I learned that when I knelt in prayer, instead of sitting in my easy chair, God often placed in my heart something I needed to know. The same evening in which Alicia talked with me about my addictions, God clarified the reasons why all of my addictive behaviors were actual sins, not just abnormal patterns. He showed me that sex was made to be within marriage, between two people. When I masturbated, I took it upon myself to have it another way besides the God-given way. That is exactly what sin is—doing my own thing my own way. The binge and purge (bulimia) on a gallon of ice cream was wrong for the same reason. God meant for food to be nourishing, to give us life. When I used food in the opposite way, it was sin. Hurting myself physically, with my whipping and cutting, was wrong. It was not treating myself with love. I needed to be kind and thoughtful to everyone. My alcohol consumption was definitely sin. The Bible speaks often against drunkenness, and that was how I drank, not a glass of wine with dinner but enough vodka to fall into bed dead drunk. To depend on anything or anyone else but God was idolatry, be it family, shopping, eating, working, drinking, etc.

I thought about the consequences of habitually practiced sin and made a firm decision that I did not want or need any of these consequences:

1.   Mind control. These addictions controlled my mind as much as my body. I wanted both body and mind controlled by God.
2.   Guilt. I wanted a sharp conscience that will keep me close to God.
3.   Dishonor. These actions were putting less value on me than the value God had placed.
4.   Lack of trust in God. Making what I thought or wanted to do of more importance than what God wanted, was idolatry. I didn't want that mentality.
5.   Shame. Choosing to do what I knew was not good for me would inevitably produce shame. This would not make me feel better or bring healing.

My eyes were opened to what I had been practicing since I had been a young child. This revelation was not guilt producing, as it might appear, but was very freeing. I didn't feel condemned. I felt more powerful, as if I had been given ammunition for the devil. He wanted to destroy me with all these addictions, and feeling guilty had never helped.

What God showed me that night clinched the beliefs in my mind. Never again did I wonder how much I could dabble in these activities and still be okay. That didn't mean I never acted on them again. They were addictions, after all, and I will probably always be tempted in these areas, but I became aware of the dangers. I knew I could ask for God's help to escape, perhaps just for the moment, but I knew His help would be present the next moment, too.

I began to see my struggles in a spiritual dimension. A war was occurring, mostly in my mind. Furthermore, I realized that everyone has similar struggles. Everyone is fighting some battle. While pondering that dilemma that all of us are in, I penned the following poem.

Bruised
(Genesis 3:15)
His heart was broken,
His soul was dried,
His bones like powder to feel,
For the Father in heaven
Forsook His own Son—
This Man was bruised in the heel.

Now crowned with thorns,
Now nailed to the cross,
Now left helpless and dead;
Made sin for us
That we might have life—
And Satan was bruised in the head.

A Wave of Grace
Self-hatred was brought so vividly to my attention. God allowed me to understand the effects it has had on my life since I was about six years old. He also let me know that I don't need this hatred as a shield around me anymore. With Alicia as my witness, I renounced the self-hatred and all of Satan's lies that came with it. I am depending on Psalm 28:7, "He is my strength, my shield from every danger" (TLB).

Hope

As I considered this self-hatred, I could understand how this could have been a central factor of why I never felt God's presence or realized His love. It was an extremely strong wall around me. As with the walls of Jericho (Joshua 6:20), only God had the ability to knock down this barrier between Himself and myself and between others and myself.

This armor had always protected me, but it had also isolated me from God and from the very people who could help me. I understood that only God could remove the armor, and if I chose to accept and thus experience God's love, the hatred would dissipate as fog does on a sunny morning. I doubted that I could actually work on it, but I knew that as I opened my heart, love would dissolve the hatred.

The entire concept was such an eye-opener, a breakthrough. Hope was sneaking in. I was excited—at three thirty in the morning! How could one short prayer have had such power? An atomic bomb just keeps exploding and exploding; that was exactly what was happening in my heart. God was at work in my life. The reverberations kept coming and coming.

———

A Wave of Grace

It is impossible to describe how I feel today: a great relief, a freeing, a bright light shining, something jarred loose. Jesus is mine and I am His. Maybe this is what peace feels like. The assurance that God is for me continues on and on. Doors and windows are being installed in the walls, letting out hatred, fear, and anger, and letting in love, peace, and hope. Oh, yes, I still hope for much more; I'm not finished yet.

———

Counselor's Note: Origins of Self-Hatred

It is a rare occasion to talk with abuse survivors and not hear them discuss their negative views about themselves. They often perceive themselves as weak, vile, and shameful. These views go back many years, to the time of childhood. Children, by nature, view themselves as the center of their world. This perspective, called egocentrism, can be violently manipulated when abuse and trauma invade a child's life. Lies told to the child become truth, that the abuse was their fault. Children exposed to abuse and violence begin to see their own vulnerabilities as the culprit, the enemy, and set out to punish this vile core at the center of their soul. Survivors of abuse begin to heal only when their views of themselves are transformed and self-acceptance takes root.

Philemon is an interesting book of the Bible, just one chapter, which I had read many times, never getting anything personal from it. I had just finished reading it again and finally understood. I was the runaway slave, rescued by Jesus and set free, to be sent back to the world, now as a slave for Jesus. Jesus not only did those things long ago for me, He continues to do so and continues to take my side, speaking up for me, not against me as I had imagined. That was what Paul did for Onesimus (verses 10–12). God desired to help and strengthen me in order to make me more usable. What was my part in the process? Allow Him to do His will. That's all I could do.

God also wanted to make me a joy to Him. Zephaniah 3:17 (NIV) reads, "The Lord your God is with you, he is mighty to save. He will take great delight in you, he will quiet you with his love, he will rejoice over you with singing." The verse was very amazing to me, especially since the prophet Zephaniah was sent to people who had turned away from God. Apparently, when people do turn back to God, as this verse says, He will rejoice over them with singing. I couldn't quite picture it yet.

So often, I would question if it were possible for me to get well. And then I'd think, *I do know it is possible.* After all, I was beginning to love people and missed them when I didn't see them for a while. I never thought I could feel that way. Love was becoming more powerful than any of the negative feelings I had. Alicia and I had been working steadily on relationships, in between other concerns that arose. Talking things out really helped me. I'd never talked as freely as I had the past few months. Pretty amazing! Another impossibility I was actually able to do! For the first time in my life, I had a voice!

Faith was arising in me. When I looked at the progress I had already made, it encouraged me. I began to think that maybe I could get through this. I was learning to pray for myself. I never did until recently; it seemed so selfish. But if I didn't learn to pray for myself, how could I pray effectively for others?

I began asking for God's help with a particular problem. He was my only hope. I prayed many times a day, telling Him what I thought and felt. I would tell Him how I hated being female. The term *female* was impersonal, more body parts than anything else; at least to me, the word presented that idea. I tried to remember to use the term *woman*— that meant a lot more than body. To me, *woman* meant all the makeup of a person: my emotions, thoughts, hopes, dreams, ideas, loves, work, qualities, etc. In therapy, I often referred to this problem, but more than a year passed before I was willing to truly deal with the issue.

> *Journal, September 3, 2012*
> *What an inspiring dream I just had! I was living in a small wooden shack, very primitive, no electricity, no inside facilities. It was cold, and I had run out of wood to burn. I was scrounging around the wooded area to pick up a few limbs when a friend came to see me. She was familiar with this place, and as we walked into the house, she showed me a door, which I had never noticed. This door opened to huge parts of the house I didn't know. Someone who had lived there before left the whole area crammed with loads of junk: furniture, knick-knacks, toys, and household items piled to the ceiling and filling all available space. She helped me carry out load after load to the dump. Then another friend came and showed me yet another door, which opened into more rooms. These rooms looked like a store, with everything new and organized and stocked with things I could use. When I began to look around, I met a mother-son team who were trying to get me out of there, the son being aggressive and pushing me, but I shoved him out of the way and kept looking. The house needed*

> *lots of repairs everywhere. Doors were missing and even*
> *some walls were plastic sheeting instead of boards.*

When I woke up, I was excited. This was the story of my life. I was living in a little shack (psychologically) and ran out of my own resources to tend to even that little bit. Then a friend came—Tom—who showed me all the "junk" that had to be removed. We worked together on this for three years. Then another friend came—Alicia—who opened rooms of usable wares and presented me with unimaginable gifts for life. There was still a lot of work to do to make the place livable. As his character is, the devil came to push me away from all that God has for me, but I shoved him out and continued inspecting my house. Proverbs 14:1 (NIV) says, "The wise woman builds her house."

One Sunday at church, someone prayed one of the most amazing prayers I've ever received. She prayed that I would realize who I am and that the Spirit would reveal to me how precious to God and loved I am. Alicia told me once that I probably have felt God's presence but just didn't recognize it. I think I did during that prayer. It was the first time I could sense God and was so thrilled.

> *Journal, September 5, 2012*
> *Something strange just happened. I was sitting here thinking that God must really care for me. Suddenly it was as if I were on God's lap, my back leaning against His chest. His arms went around me for a few minutes.*
> *Then He said, "I love you."*
> *A minute later, I replied, "I love You, too."*
> *"Is there anything else you need to know?"*
> *"No."*
> *That was the end. God loves me. There's not much more I really need to know.*

A Wave of Grace
Thank You, Lord. Thank You, Lord, for the assurance of your love. You are so good to me.

Celebrate Recovery

In October, I went to a yard sale where I saw information about Celebrate Recovery, a self-help group that works with people who have problems with hurts, habits, and hang-ups. When I expressed that I was a recovering alcoholic, I was invited to attend. From the first meeting, I received more insight and enjoyed it more than any other group I had ever attended as an alcoholic. This group is similar to Alcoholics Anonymous but with a much more spiritual emphasis. The twelve principles are based on scripture, and recovery is attributed to Jesus Christ and the redemption He bought for us on the cross. After a few weeks, I asked someone to be my sponsor. She and I worked through the steps, and then I began helping someone else work through the same steps.

Celebrate Recovery's steps are a progression from denial to having a need for God, and from becoming willing to have His help all the way to passing this good news to others who need the same help. The year-long study, which is taught annually, instructs how to repent and ask God for forgiveness, how to confess our faults and make amends with others, how to receive grace and new life, and how to live with gratitude and a giving spirit.

───── ᨎᨎᨎ᯼᯼᯼᯼ ─────

A Wave of Grace

Celebrate Recovery has been another gift of God's grace to me. I've made some good friends, people I love and who love me. I keep getting amazed at how God works. He stirs my heart and then drops something special into my life. His addition might be a bit of wisdom, a new friend, or an extra hope or joy, just anything that will bless and help me on my journey.

───── ᨎᨎᨎ᯼᯼᯼᯼ ─────

The following poem was written immediately after a church service in the fall of 2012. Every Sunday, when communion is given, the members kneel at the altar to receive the sacraments (bread and wine). It is always a time of praise and thanksgiving. On this particular Sunday, I was very touched by God's Spirit:

Communion
His blood gushed out through head and face;
That blood can blot, wipe, and erase.
Though volumes fell that ghastly day,
One drop has washed my sins away.
Blood from His back and from His side
Gives me the strength to walk, abide.
That precious blood—I finally knew,
One drop would give me life anew.

Journal, October 16, 2012
At the end of the counseling session today, Alicia prayed
a wonderful prayer. She told God that she knew He cared
for me and that He knew she cared for me. That's an
astonishing thought!

Intentional Living

Tom had often mentioned intentional living and acting. After about a year of working with Alicia, one day, while reading an historical biography, I realized I had not been intentional the past few weeks, just kind of floating along on the bliss I felt. Life was not very successful with this attitude, I noticed, so I listed some ideas to help me live more intentionally:

- Keep busy at home—no sitting for long periods.
- Memorize sections of scripture.
- Exercise often.
- Shower daily.
- Attend Celebrate Recovery at least once each week.
- Spend time with a friend once or twice a week.
- Keep my house clean.
- Keep a close guard on my addictive behaviors.

- Call my Celebrate Recovery sponsor daily.
- Take medications as prescribed.
- Treat myself kindly.
- Keep journaling.
- Continue counseling with Alicia.
- Do a daily act of kindness.

I knew I couldn't do all of these all the time, but these were goals and something concrete I could use to check on myself to see how I was doing.

When I read the previous list of intentional living ideas to Alicia, she challenged me to list ways I could treat myself kindly, as I had stated I wanted to do. Here were some suggestions for myself:

- Wear jewelry and lipstick when leaving the house.
- Laugh out loud at the antics of my dogs and cats.
- Talk to God about what I think and feel.
- Think about the characteristics that cause others to like me.
- Tell myself daily that, through Jesus Christ, I am clean in God's sight.
- Remember that since I want to love others, I must love myself, too.
- Ask God to help me make good choices.
- Have healthy foods in the house.
- Sometimes do what I want to do simply because I want to, not because I need to.
- Eliminate activities that I don't need to do and don't enjoy.
- Keep a balance in my life: God, others, work, play, rest.
- Don't call myself ugly names ever again.

These were not hard-and-fast rules but general guidelines that helped make my life easier and more pleasant.

A Blessed Home

My house didn't feel like home. I had lived here three years and still didn't like it. I was not afraid, but I just didn't feel comfortable and I wondered why. Alicia and I discussed this a couple of times, and finally I had some insight. While I was growing up, the house was not a pleasant place. In Chicago, I always rented, so the houses were never mine. In Minnesota, my home wasn't safe from Pastor Bill. Here in Alabama, I did not own a place until I married. During our marriage, the house didn't seem safe with Wayne there, not that he was unkind or abusive in any way, but he was simply present. Perhaps the sixty years of not feeling safe is the reason I was not at home in my own home. A second possible reason was that while living in my home, I had often acted out on my addictions. Behaviors like those did not lead to God's presence.

I talked about my home with some friends at church. Five women were willing to meet at my place for a house blessing. They prayed over each room and sprinkled blessed water everywhere. All uncleanness was prayed out. I carried a candle to each room, signifying the darkness fleeing and Jesus the Light entering (John 1:9). All five were real prayer warriors, who prayed mostly for me, that I might truly know God and know how much He loved me. The blessing was so special. I didn't imagine it would be such a holy experience.

Being Okay

A friend recommended the book *No Stones*, by Marnie C. Ferree, and as I read it, the author reached deep inside of me, dug out every thought or feeling I'd ever had about my abuse, somehow translated these thoughts and feelings into words, and printed them in her book. Furthermore, I realized that Alicia also did that week after week. She, too, reached down into me, pulled up all kinds of rottenness, and translated it not only into words but also into caring. As *No Stones* indicated, shame was the killer. Alicia told me about shame so many times and that I must avoid behaviors that caused that result. She said that without sobriety in every area of life, I would never get well. Only when I had that secure, would I be able to work on the underlying issues of abuse and abandonment.

This permeating sense of shame had always been present, always. Originally, Pastor Bill and my family members should have borne that shame, not me. Later, the shame resulted from my own actions. It was all redeemed though. On the cross, Jesus was naked when He carried all of our sins. His shame must have been tremendous. When He took my sins and weaknesses, He bore my shame, too, and I didn't need to carry it anymore. It is not who I am. Jesus redeemed me from that. I am His child and precious in His sight.

Shame was not my identity anymore. Other parts were emerging and taking over. Sometimes I saw bits of something but was not sure what it was, maybe that I was becoming comfortable in my own skin. I began to feel as if I belonged inside of me, as if I were Nancy, and that was okay. The first awareness of becoming one person was so exciting. Alicia's insistence that I speak in first person was the initial step. The pieces of me were fitting together some way as if being put into one big puzzle. A year later, I was almost integrated, and still another year later, I was a whole person.

Feeling lost and alone was a common emotion for me, even though I had not recognized it until I worked with Alicia for a year. It was true. In my early years, I had been abandoned in many ways, and for most of my life, I had been imprisoned in my inner isolation. I did not realize I was lonely, but I always knew I was alone. Remembering how Jesus was abandoned by His friends and even, at a critical time in His life, by His own parent, was helpful in dealing with this desolate feeling. He was very aware of me. I wasn't alone anymore. "How precious it is, Lord, to realize that you are thinking about me constantly! I can't even count how many times a day your thoughts turn towards me" (Psalms 139:17 TLB).

I never stopped at an adult store but was often very tempted on the way to Chicago to visit relatives. There were several well-advertised ones along the way, and I wanted to stop but didn't, because I knew that even if I didn't buy anything, those pictures would be in my mind forever. I was learning how to care for my mind, which was an important step in the process of recovery. Watching what I allowed in my spirit was even more important than what I allowed in my body.

Counselor's Note: Sex Addiction and Trauma

In her book, *No Stones*, therapist and author Marnie Ferree wrote, "Every sex addict I've known or treated has experienced some form of abandonment. Every single one" (p.139). Abandonment and sexual abuse during childhood can create an exploited sense of sexuality along with toxic shame that settles deep in the soul beyond the sufferer's conscious awareness. It's like a soul-sickness that influences choices, feelings, and priorities. Just like someone with a broken bone can only focus on feeling better, someone with abuse-induced soul-sickness can only focus on alleviating that damaged sexuality. The pain becomes even more unbearable when pornography is used to relieve the pain. Pornography provides a short-term fix where exploited sexuality becomes normalized and even desirable, yet the experience further drives home the distorted sense of self. Only when the sufferer removes the addictions can the deeper pain of abuse and trauma be addressed and ultimately healed.

No longer was it just Alicia explaining again and again why I needed to be sober (addiction free) in all areas of my life. The desire became mine. I wanted to live clean, to be God-controlled, not addiction-controlled. This desire was partly to avoid the negative consequences of addictive living, but I had three more powerful reasons:

- to live with Christ in me (Colossians 1:27)
- to walk in the Spirit (Galatians 5:16)
- to have confidence before Jesus (1 John 2:28)

Looking at godly people, I became able to understand what they were doing and even to incorporate some of their skills into my own life. This ability surprised me since, until then, I had never been able to discern anything about people: what they were doing, their intentions, or the meaning of their gestures and facial expressions. I was learning from others and gaining insight.

———ᜒᜒᜒᜒ᠊ᜒᜒᜒ᠊ᜒᜒᜒ———

A Wave of Grace

I am not discouraged in the struggle, but it's scary to think how strong the evil within me is. That's the exact reason, though, why I am in desperate need of Jesus and His cleansing and power. I have no other recourse. Thank You, Jesus, for being with me, for being on my side, for being willing to go to the cross for me. Thank You for Your life and light which is replacing my death and darkness.

———ᜒᜒᜒᜒ᠊ᜒᜒᜒ᠊ᜒᜒᜒ———

Great thankfulness began to flood my whole being nearly all the time. I saw how God had blessed me and praised Him constantly for lifting me out of the oppression, for rescuing me from myself, for supporting and protecting me, and for bringing life to me. As a response of gratitude, I wrote this poem.

Poem to God
Dear God and loving Father of us all,
Dear Savior, Lord, the One who died for me,
The One who shed Your all-atoning blood,
Here is my praise, confession, and my plea.

You brought me life when surely there was none,
When death surrounded and had penned me in.
You gave Your strength and healing in a touch
And brought back hope into this heart again.

So seldom do I recognize Your voice;
So seldom do I realize Your love.
Forgive my hardened heart and make it soft;
Bring me the peace that comes from You above.

The burdens that I carried on my own,
The struggles that I let tear You from me,
The wish to run my life in my own way,
Forgive, oh God, and make me truly free.

Let unforgiveness, callousness, and pride
Wash out until I'm finally clean and pure.
Help me desire to be what pleases You;
Help me desire to stand strong and endure.

I gave to You, and You took up the yoke
And bore the burden that was mine alone;
You took it all—the sorrow and the shame,
The load of sin which You should never own.

You touched my life, my soul, my mind, my all;
In every circumstance You led the way.
In every situation gave me good,
Much more than human tongue could ever say.

Just as I am You made me; all is well.
Ever and always You will do what's best.
In You and only You is love and joy,
And hope and healing, inner peace and rest.

Support and refuge, everlasting arms
Are underneath, to comfort and to guide;
Above, Your wings to keep safe and protect,
And Your sweet presence all along my side.

Dear God and loving Father of us all,
Dear Savior, Lord, the One who died for me,
The One who shed Your all-atoning blood,
Here is my praise, confession, and my plea.

One day, two friends came for me and we picked up another friend, ate breakfast at our favorite restaurant, and spent the day together. It was wonderful! This was the first time when I went out with friends that I didn't feel inferior or left out. What a great feeling! I said anything I wanted to say and was treated as an equal. We were all equal. We went where anyone suggested and stayed as long as anyone wanted to stay, then went to the next place when someone said, "Let's go there." I never had an experience like that before and didn't know I could relate so well with others. It was the most fun I had ever had, the best day of my life!

——⁓⁓⊙⊙⊙——

A Wave of Grace
The day with friends is so special, a wonderful gift from God. It gives me a great boost of confidence that God is continuing His work.

——⁓⁓⊙⊙⊙——

On my first time through Grace Group, I had been introduced to a lot of helpful material that I had not been able to absorb, so I signed up for the journey again. I understood a lot more the second time because I was less fearful and had much anticipation. I was becoming aware of God's working in my heart, changing attitudes and desires. Jane was an amazing woman. I learned so much about God and how He operated in people through her praying and by her total love and acceptance of me. Two major breakthroughs occurred: shame and contempt were worked out of my heart, and I felt the first twinge of desire to settle my gender issue in a godly manner. Again, Alicia and I reviewed and discussed each lesson. This was such a boost to my spiritual and psychological well-being.

After the second time with Grace Group, I thought I might want to help by coleading, so I went to Texas to receive training; I have assisted the group twice. I was not very skilled at recognizing how the Holy Spirit wanted me to respond, but Jane taught me about dealing with people and depending on God. We worked together closely. I had a wonderful opportunity to pour into others what had been poured into me.

As each session of Grace Group began, I was again made aware of how broken most people are and how few discover God's grace in the midst of their brokenness. I was thinking about this one late summer day while I was mowing my lawn, and I was inspired to write the following poem:

Broken People
We're broken people, bowed with awful grief;
Broken people, but there is relief.
We're broken people, hoping pain will cease;
Broken people, but there is God's peace.
We're broken people, scared to look above;
Broken people, but there is God's love.
We're broken people, suffering shame and loss;
Broken people, but we know the cross.
We're broken people, who just grasp and grope;
Broken people, who now have some hope.
We're broken people, filled with great disgrace;
Broken people, who have found God's grace.

Alicia's godly wisdom affected my thinking, as Tom's had done. I was like a flower garden. Tom had tilled the soil and applied fertilizer. Now Alicia planted the seeds and watched as the plants grew and the buds developed. I was very excited to see so many flowers in such an array of beautiful colors. The following journal entry is one of the appearing blooms:

> *Journal, April 26, 2013*
> *Psalm 18:19 (NIV) reads, "He rescued me because he delighted in me." According to this verse, God delighted in me first, and because of His delight, He then rescued me. How could He delight in me the way I was? I'm not all that great even now. That means I do not need to perform, for Him to be happy with me. Since I always thought I had to work like a dog to live a Christian life, I appreciate this important point. He actually delights in me just because I am.*

In June 2013, I became officially retired. For someone who put up a big fuss against having any celebration, I certainly enjoyed the retirement party. Many students, former students, teachers, and other friends came to wish me happiness. I was very surprised and enjoyed visiting with them all so much. Pictures of my life were displayed, along with a mat allowing visitors to write me a message. The cake was gorgeous, decorated with edible crayons along the edges; it was delicious and rich. Several of my friends planned and organized this reception. Someone even made a video for me. The afternoon was so special.

The high school graduation was the following evening. I was honored then, too, for the thirty-three years I had taught there. A dozen long-stemmed yellow roses (my favorite rose) and a plaque with my favorite verse (2 Corinthians 9:8) were presented to me, along with a generous gift of cash. God had truly blessed me by bringing me to this school. I was sure I would never have survived anywhere else. I made some good friends and planned to keep contact with them.

A Wave of Grace

The honor given to me during the reception and graduation was totally mind-boggling. Yes, I had taught for many years, but for most of this time, I was not confident or aware of how people viewed me. I couldn't brush this off as easily as I usually do. I begin to understand how loved I am.

Being a Woman

Journal, August 1, 2013
This was today's prayer: Thank You, God, for the beautiful world You created for us to enjoy and use. Thank You for the animals and birds, the flowers and trees. Thank You for the seashores, mountains, and forests. Thank You for the stars, sun, and moon. Thank You for the oceans and rivers, the farms and prairies. It's all good.

Thank You for the people in my life—my family members and friends. Thank You for creating each one.

> *Then, Lord, how can I be so crass as to think You did not know what you were doing when You made me? How can I stand in front of You and accuse You of being mistaken about me? That You goofed? Forgive me for doing just that very thing all my years. Thank You for making me as I am, a woman. You do not make mistakes. You always know and do what is best at all times (Ephesians 1:8 TLB). I rejoice in Your unfailing ability. I not only want to act right; I also want to believe right and think right. Thank You for making me as I am. Amen.*
>
> *What did I just pray? Did I thank God for my being a woman? How is that possible?*

Alicia and I had been working together for almost two years. I liked being in her office. While there, I was who I wanted to be, said what I want to say, saw my life in another perspective, tried on new thoughts, hoped for something different, and dreamed big dreams. Although we had touched on many areas, there were two primary issues: addictions and gender. I struggled with addictions the entire time with Alicia, and even though I became nearly addiction free, this will most likely continue to trouble me for the rest of my life.

The gender issue was different. I did not realize that my dissatisfaction was a problem. All my life I hated being who I was made to be. From an early age, I wanted to be a boy. It seemed safer. Birthday cake candles were blown out with that wish. The first star in the night sky was wished upon with the same hope. That was even my desire when I got the big half of a chicken's wishbone. As I matured physically, I loathed my body. I absolutely detested having to wear a dress every day to teach. Alicia and I talked and talked and talked about this. Week after week, I'd say essentially the same words, "I hate being a woman, and I know God doesn't like this attitude." But I kept talking, and eventually there were several breakthroughs:

1. I was not willing to accept being a woman, but if God would make me willing, I would agree to it.
2. I became willing to change my attitude.
3. I was grudgingly accepting of my gender but definitely did not like it.
4. I learned to accept who I was, in general.

5. I thanked God, without totally realizing what I said, for being who He made me.
6. I became happy being the woman God made me to be.

These steps took about a year to complete. Never once did Alicia suggest that we had already discussed this problem fifty times. She knew I wanted to break free and encouraged me all the way, rejoicing with each small step.

—◦◦◦◦◦◦◦—

A Wave of Grace
Thank the good Lord. What a step this is! And all because of God's grace. He is doing something I cannot do, and it is thrilling!

—◦◦◦◦◦◦◦—

Congratulations were due! It had been exactly one year since I drank alcohol. True, I had had over twenty years of sobriety earlier, but I was on the wagon again. In addition, I had either totally put down or greatly reduced my acting on all the other addictions.

Forgiven and Forgiving

I still had some trouble with two addictions. With most sins, I was not *doing* what God wanted me to *do*, but with these, I was not *being* who God wanted me to *be*. I didn't want to hide from God anymore, or be separated from Him, or keep approaching Him with shame. I decided I wanted to live clean before Him. He will give me the strength I need, without my cowering or begging. I could ask God boldly and without fear (Hebrews 4:16), and He will bring His power to help me.

I began to like myself and didn't have a need to hurt myself anymore. All my life I had hated Nancy and was so angry with her, but the intense hatred and anger against her was dissipating. I knew I still had badness within me but also goodness. I was trying to see myself as the Bible says God sees me.

As I reread *The Wounded Heart* by Dan B. Allender, recommended by the Grace Group workbook, I began to understand how I had sinned against God and others, in response to my abuse:

- did not trust God
- built walls to avoid people
- did not love or care for others
- did not look to God to meet my needs
- put hope in temporal instead of eternal
- hardened my heart against the needs of others
- did not appreciate who God made me to be
- refused to be vulnerable to God or anyone else
- refused to share my heart
- lived only to protect myself
- agreed with Satan on many lies
- accepted addictions to relieve pain

When I considered this list of my sins against God and people, I found it much easier to forgive those who had sinned against me. I could forgive them, knowing that God had totally forgiven me. Such a freeing experience!

———⁓⁓⁓———

A Wave of Grace
Forgiving is a God thing. Because His sacrifice provided forgiveness and freedom for me, I can respond by passing on the same forgiveness to others. It is wonderful to discern God placing His characteristics into my mind and heart. "And I pray that Christ will be more and more at home in your hearts, living within you as you trust in him" (Ephesians 3:17 TLB).

———⁓⁓⁓———

I thought a lot about how I felt as a woman. To my surprise, I liked it. Besides the months of counseling sessions, I thought of something else that had been helpful. I could finally visualize several strong women who were part of my life. I used to think that all women were weak, wishy-washy doormats, and I didn't want any part of it. Another fallacy I believed is that strong people didn't have problem areas or quirks and that they could do and be everything. With that definition, of course, I didn't know any strong people. I learned the truth and realized that the strong women I have had as my friends have been remarkable role models for many years. More and more I enjoyed being the woman that God made me to be.

———ᴡᴏᴏᴏᴇᴏᴏ———

A Wave of Grace

Psalm 55:18 says, "He hath delivered my soul in peace from the battle that was against me." God has delivered me from this great battle that raged against my soul for sixty years. The gender issue was a huge block standing between God and me. It is crumbled to the ground, and who I am in Christ is rising from the broken pieces.

———ᴡᴏᴏᴏᴇᴏᴏ———

Counselor's Note: Gender and Trauma

Many adults survivors of sexual abuse grow up with a distorted view of gender. They see their maleness or femaleness as being the reason they were abused. This is partly due to the egocentric perspective of children that age, but mostly this bias occurs because it was their vulnerability, their sexuality, that was exploited and exposed. Abuse triggers an instinctual fight/flight response, both in the body and in the mind. Anything and anyone that can be labeled as a danger will be, in order to protect and preserve oneself. If being female is seen as the threat, then the mind will turn on that and hate it. This gender hatred is similar to an autoimmune disorder where the body's natural defenses mistake the body for bacteria and attack it. Over time, Nancy began to view her femininity with new eyes and eventually learned to accept and embrace her own vulnerability, not as the cause of her abuse but as a God-given part of being human.

Alicia often mentioned that we are both good and bad, and I could now understand the concept. We were created in God's image (Genesis 1:27), "fearfully and wonderfully made" (Psalm 139:14). Yet "What is man, that thou art mindful of him?" (Psalm 8:4) and "If we say that we have no sin, we deceive ourselves" (1 John 1:8). It was not hard anymore to see myself both ways. What was still difficult for me to comprehend was that God looked at me the same way when I was doing well and when I was not. It was easy to feel that He would think less of me when I did poorly and more of me when I did better. There are many verses, though, that offer God's everlasting love and mercy. If He was going to love me only when I was good, how was it that He sent Jesus when I was so unlovely? Jesus surely knew I would need forgiveness more than once. If I am instructed in Matthew 18:21-22 to forgive others seventy times seven, I'm assured God will go far beyond that.

God had aided me in so many other ways, too, in addition to forgiveness. I loved the book of Psalms because the writers expressed their thoughts and feelings so eloquently. "Yes, he alone is my rock, my rescuer, defense and fortress. Why then should I be tense with fear when troubles come? All those who know your mercy, Lord, will count on you for help. For you have never yet forsaken those who trust in you" (Psalms 62:2, 9:10 TLB). The following poem was written when I finally knew that God truly is for me, not against me (Psalms 56:9).

Psalm 121:2
The Lord who made the heavens and earth
Stoops low to meet my need;
The One who put the stars in space
Has promised help indeed.
It's not an "if" He comes to me,
No "maybe" He'll arrive,
The God who hung the planets out,
That God is still alive.
He helps where He is welcomed in;
His promises are true.
The hand He offers me each day,
He offers now to you.

6

Grace for Today
(Age Sixty-Nine)

The Future

Many times Alicia encouraged me to reach out when I didn't want to, and now I have a large support system: church, Grace Group, Alicia, Celebrate Recovery, school friends, and other friends. Every part is helping in my continuing recovery. This is the entire Psalm 55:18, "He hath delivered my soul in peace from the battle that was against me: for there were many with me."

There was no way, if I had continued struggling by myself, that I would be where I am today. Alicia has told me many times, "We are hurt in relationships, and we are healed in relationships." For five years, Tom and Alicia dangled the carrot of relationships in front of me. I thank God for them and for their commitment and wise words.

Until recently, hopes and dreams had never been a part of my life. My goal was to survive one day at a time, and often I didn't even have that goal. Having no hope is not really living. One day Alicia asked me a question.

"Why don't you ever talk about the future?"

Pause. "The future? Ahhhhh, I never thought about it."

This answer initiated many lively discussions about what I wanted to do with the rest of my life. At first, I couldn't think of much, but over the next month, as I became conscious of the future, a lot of thoughts interested me. Alicia encouraged me to make a binder for my new ideas. I did, and I have five categories, which I keep developing: Care of Self, Writing, Ministries, Projects/Activities, and Social. Right now, I have many more interests than I can possible do. Since I retired, I must be careful not to get involved with everything that catches my eye. I constantly have to make hard decisions about how I spend my time and what I most want and need to do.

The Ministries category is the hardest to manage. So many places desperately need volunteers. At this time, I am involved in as many areas as I am able to handle. Here are some of the ways I serve:

- cook twice a month for twenty people in Celebrate Recovery
- teach a lesson occasionally for Celebrate Recovery
- colead a small weekly "step study" group with Celebrate Recovery
- colead the Grace Group study two or three times a year
- help prepare and serve breakfast for the homeless once a month
- price and help with Celebrate Recovery's yard sales several times a year
- help older friends with their special needs

God has been very good to me. He is more real than ever before. I have learned to trust Him and love Him and others. I have such a peace and quietness within. No pill or magic action will bring healing. Alicia says that very few will take recovery to the end; most just want relief from a stressful crisis, and when that occurs, they are satisfied with that little bit and quit. My entire process so far has been God-directed. I was not even aware of His continual work until recently. Now I see His hand in everything.

The Process of Self-Acceptance

Occasionally, someone asks why it took so long for me to feel that I had value and worth. The process did not seem long to me, maybe because I never thought of it as a goal, and, in fact, I never imagined it. As self-acceptance began to happen, I was very surprised. Even today, I am quite amazed that I am able to like and enjoy myself. It did take several years of counseling and hard work, and now I understand the reasons:

- *Abandonment.*
  This is the overriding reason. As an infant and a child, I never bonded with my parents, and this connection is essential for trust, and then relationships, to flourish. I have discovered that one learns to accept herself only within an accepting relationship. This is the formula: Bond/Connect + Trust + Relationship = Self-Acceptance and Worth. It takes a long time to unlearn distrust and to learn to bond with someone enough to have a real relationship.

- *Length of time before receiving help.*
  Being in my sixties before receiving the help I needed means that I sat with the knowledge of being alone and unprotected for a long time. Early experiences literally wired my brain in a particular pattern. The good news is that these patterns can be changed, even later in life; however, the change requires hundreds of nurturing experiences over a lengthy time.

- *Spiritual abuse.*
  From the beginning, I had a warped view of God, from both the church in which I was raised (very legalistic) and my father (whom most young children view as God). Pastor Bill's abuse in Minnesota strongly reinforced my skewed viewpoint. If only my mind were involved, the matter could be resolved in a brief time by memorizing pertinent Bible verses and listening to praise music. The main issue, however, was trust, and trust takes time.

- *Addictions.*
  Addictive behaviors inevitably produce shame, and shame brings hatred and disgust for self. Of the four reasons why my self-worth took so long in coming, this is the only one I could actually work on. This is why Alicia was firm in her requirement that I must stop all addictive behaviors and why she was so encouraging of every baby step I took in the right direction. I find that I cannot let up, even a little, or the shame and hatred return. It grieves me to say that sometimes I do what I want to do, even though I know it's wrong, even though I know I will later hate myself, and even though I know God would give me the power to resist if I asked Him.

All I can do is fall back on God's grace. His love and mercy are everlasting. My hope is in Him. I pray more earnestly and look to Him more intently. When I do slip into an old pattern, confessing it to a mentor (I have several) and discussing how I can return to God are helpful. I want more than behavioral sobriety.

This poem was written one pretty spring day when I was driving about one hundred miles to visit a friend. She was a shut-in but was always happy and thankful. I thought, *I want a grace mindset, too, so that when good comes my way, or bad, I will still stand firm.*

Romans 5:20
"We have access by faith into this grace wherein we stand."
We stand in grace, when all feels lost.
God gave this grace at what a cost!
We stand in grace when nights are bleak,
When silence reigns, and we can't speak.
We stand in grace when joy is gone,
And we can't live without its song.
We stand in grace when skies are gray,
When hope is lost, and we can't pray.
We stand in grace when hearts hold fear,
And we don't feel Your presence near.

And we still stand when winter's past,
When roses spread their blooms at last.
And we still stand when trees are green,
When robins sing, and spring is seen.
And we still stand when winds are calm,
And tender grace becomes our balm.
And we still stand when peace is here,
When doubts are gone, and God is near.
God's grace fails not; it's strong and true.
On grace we stand; it takes us through.

New Insights

As I talk with Christians who are more mature than I, they all admit that they have flaws in their life that cause them sorrow. When I first heard this, I couldn't believe it. I had so little awareness of real life that I thought strong Christians got past that point and could live on top of everything. As I read the scriptures, I understood that this was never so. We always have a desperate need for Jesus. In fact, I think the stronger my faith gets, the more I need Him. As I walk more in the Spirit, instead of in my own strength, I must lean more on Jesus. I not only need His gifts; I need Him.

Thankfully, I am learning to lean on God. He is my hope. I am learning that when tough times come, they are part but not all of life. Somehow, I can and do get through. A hard place is only a temporary position, not a permanent stop. Isaiah 43:2 says, "When you go through deep waters and great trouble, I will be with you. When you go through rivers of difficulty, you will not drown! When you walk through the fire of oppression, you will not be burned up—the flames will not consume you" (TLB). God says that we will go *through* all of these difficulties.

My perspective on the past is constantly changing. I now understand the reason for many of my feelings and actions. Just recently, I realized why I have never been able to express emotions and, for most of my life, why I didn't think I had any. One brother was physically cruel to me, as well as sexually abusive. The cruelty was much more pervasive, and I learned very early not to react. Because a reaction would bring more cruelty, I swallowed all anger and fear. He was all I had. Even at four and five years old, I wouldn't tell on him. I didn't want him later taking his punishment out on me. Whatever he did, I couldn't let it matter. It was either take him as he was or be completely alone. Now I can feel what I did not dare to feel then.

One day, the fall after I retired, I was helping a teacher at my school, when I suddenly saw the experiences of my brother's cruelty in a new light. What happened to me is why I always stuck up for the underdogs in every class I taught. Although I did not understand myself, I could understand the child who was teased or who had no confidence or who was withdrawn. They were the ones who received my extra attention, praise, and encouragement. They were the ones I called upon to do special jobs or to lead spelling. I found ways to honor them in front of their classmates, so that the other students would, hopefully, see them differently. I did this instinctively. Now I know why I could spot a child who was discouraged or a loner. I loved those children the most. Yes, I did have favorites, but they were not the popular kids or the ones who gave the most expensive Christmas gifts. My favorites were the ones who leaned on me when I was at their desk helping with a math problem. The ones whose hair had not been fixed that morning or who gave me a pencil instead of a twenty-five-dollar gift card. It's true that I didn't like adults much, but I loved the children.

My heart is full of praise now, as I realize again how God was redeeming my past all along. My brother mistreated me for about ten years, but God has been redeeming me for thirty-three years! The positive was three times the negative! It's thrilling to realize that, in my desperate need, I could still meet the needs of other desperate ones. Alicia frequently suggested that I look for Jesus in my early experiences. She told me again when I was describing my brother's actions. God himself revealed to me exactly how He was not only *with* me but was actually working *through* me. What a peace and joy this brings!

Now I understand why I had so much relational difficulty even before the Minnesota years. This adds to the reasons why I always worked so hard, why I was indifferent to people, why I couldn't trust, why I withdrew and produced the red-brick building. Abandonment, sexual abuse, and physical cruelty wired my brain. I am not responsible for what others did.

I am responsible, though, for much of the chaos in my life. I am responsible for the choices I made to continue living in that mindset and for the addictions that I've picked up. As I work on changing my life and on trusting God and safe people, my brain pathways are finding new routes. Age doesn't matter here. Hope is fantastic and will do wonders in a person's heart and mind. Yes, it takes a while; sometimes it takes a long time, but so what? Life gets better and better all along the way.

God helps me *today* because He is "I AM" (Exodus 3:14). Jesus said He *is* (present tense) the God of Abraham, Isaac, and Jacob (Matthew 22:32), not *was* (past tense) their God. My only hope and peace is present right now. That is what Emmanuel means, too, "God with us" (Matthew 1:23). God is not just some pie-in-the-sky idea. He wants to be my God for today, for whatever comes today. I am learning to trust Him, learning that He is good and loving. He wants to fill me with His joy and hope, and He wants me to look to Him for help in every situation. This now rests and resides in my heart.

While writing *Endless Waves*, I reviewed everything with Alicia. This project was very therapeutic. Scores of items and words I used were discussed together. I received clarity on many perplexing things. We had had conversations about the Bible school in Minnesota so many times that I thought it was a buried subject, but, as I wrote about it, I learned that the topic was still heavy in my heart. I had never made an emotional connection to that part of my story, and, until I grasped the reality and truth of Pastor Bill's spiritual and sexual damage of me, I would not enjoy thorough recovery and healing. Early one morning, I pursued the emotional side of his abuse. The journal I wrote was revealing to me. Because it is long, I placed it at the back of *Endless Waves* under the title *Notes*.

What I Did and Still Do

Since others so often ask me what I did to get to where I am today, I will list things that have been helpful. These are my things only and certainly are not given as advice for anyone else. The list is long, for I was very serious about healing and have worked diligently. I have applied some of the items for several years, while others I have incorporated only recently. I practice all of them now and plan to continue.

- *Got professional Christian counseling.*
  My insurance did not cover any of my five years of Christian counseling, yet I knew the need was critical enough for the sacrifice.
- *Desired God.*
  I knew He was the only One who could pull me out of the pit, and I still know He has the resources and willingness to help in every situation.
- *Stayed in for the long haul.*
  I wanted complete healing and deliverance, no matter how long it took. It has taken longer than I planned, but the recovery is far more complete than I ever imagined, too.

- *Listened to the counselors.*

  When I began to trust Tom and Alicia, I did what they suggested. After all, they were doing better than I was. One day it occurred to me, *Since I think I am so stupid, why do I listen only to myself and not to others?*

- *Began a social life.*

  This took quite a while to get started. Now every close friend I have is trustworthy and directs me in godly paths. All others have been regulated to acquaintance level. I spend one or two times a week with friends. Good relationships bring healing. Even God realized that Adam needed someone besides Himself (Genesis 2:20–22).

- *Attended Celebrate Recovery.*

  Because I was not very comfortable with people, Alicia had to push me a good bit at first, but now I see the value of support groups. As I get more involved, I have an increasing number of supportive friends who love and help me toe the line.

- *Spent daily time with God.*

  I learned to read the Bible for relationship, not just facts. I pray throughout the day, talking to God about my joys and problems. Memorizing scripture, with the intent of placing it in my *heart*, has also helped me.

- *Found a church.*

  This needed to be a place where the Bible is balanced in its preaching and teaching, where basic doctrines are taught and not skewed in one area or another. I also wanted the people to be friendly and accepting.

- *Became addiction free.*

  This was not easy. After about a year of humbling myself and talking with Alicia every week about my slipups, the hold that addictions had on me began to relent. She never scolded or coddled me, just listened, gave helpful advice, and often prayed with me.

- *Gave myself leeway.*
  I was too hard on myself, but I did learn that perfection is not the goal. I can be patient and kind. This takes time and someone to help.
- *Picked my battles.*
  I cannot address every problem at the same time. I deal with one or two main issues, sometimes for six months or more, until they loosen their hold, then I choose another pressing area until free, etc.
- *Kept a journal.*
  I never write every day, but when something is on my mind, I write everything I can think about it, day after day, until my mind is clear.
- *Forgave myself and others.*
  I found this process long and hard to begin with, but my bitterness had me bound to the abusers. The freedom of release is well worth the self-denial.
- *Owned pets and plants.*
  I find such joy and unconditional love from my dogs and cats. Over the years, I've had rabbits, guinea pigs, hedgehogs, finches, canaries, a pot-bellied pig, turtles, and hamsters. It all is fun. I always have green plants and flowers to brighten the house and yard.
- *Read, read, read.*
  I find most of my helpful books at thrift stores and yard sales, and during the last few years I have read fifty or sixty books that spoke directly to my need at the time. I underlined and wrote questions, then discussed them with Tom or Alicia. This was a huge part of my healing.
- *Avoided mind junk.*
  I am extremely careful what I read, watch, and listen to. My mind won't heal if I flood it with bad language, sex, and violence.

- *Gave thanks.*
  For a long time I kept a little book where I would write three things for which I was thankful that day. It's become a habit, and I thank God daily for little blessings.
- *Kept hope alive.*
  It took me five years to learn, but like David in the Bible, I can speak encouraging words to my own heart (Psalm 28:7, 34:4, 40:1–2, 61:2, 103:1–2). One of my favorite sayings is "It is okay to not be okay."
- *Took care of self.*
  I am eating healthier, taking medications as prescribed, keeping doctor appointments, and getting regular sleep. Exercise is still a weak point, but I am very active.
- *Volunteered.*
  I need to be giving just as I have been receiving. I chose a few service projects I enjoy, but I am careful not to get swamped or let others pressure me into more than I can comfortably handle.
- *Confessed my sins and weaknesses.*
  As I confessed weekly to Alicia, I became more and more sensitive to my sin, and the desire to practice it became less and less. This confession was not for forgiveness but for the brokenness that leads to restoration. James 5:16 says, *"Make this a common practice: Confess your sins to each other and pray for each other so that you can live together whole and healed."* (MSG)
- *Took responsibility.*
  It took a long time to realize I was *not* responsible for what was done to me. I also learned that I *was* responsible for how I responded to the abuse. Instead of turning *away* from God and into addictions, hiding, and refusing to love and forgive, I needed to allow those actions against me to turn me *toward* Him.

- *Watched godly winners.*
  It may take some looking, but they can be found. I wanted to see what made them so successful and was able to incorporate some of their secrets into my own life.
- *Set goals.*
  This doesn't mean I need to meet these specific goals in order to succeed, but, rather, the goals give a direction. I have gained much more than I ever listed or imagined.
- *Enjoyed little blessings.*
  Since big gifts do not come often in life, I look for small favors that make me happy or give satisfaction. I love dog kisses, chimes sounding in the wind, a conversation with a friend, a good book, etc.
- *Found avenues for creativity.*
  Growing plants, writing, finding solutions for house and yard questions, and other creative endeavors give such a boost to my morale. I opened myself to dormant gifts and talents.
- *Let go of "if only's"*
  Because the past is gone, I can't do much about it except learn from it. Living in the present has become more exciting than living in the past.
- *Took color pictures.*
  Although my tendency has always been to view people and situations in black and white, I am noticing that real life is seldom that cut and dried. Now I can enjoy people even with their flaws, because I am aware that others enjoy me with all of my flaws.
- *Realized freedom.*
  The truth of God's Word says I am free. "And you shall know the truth, and the truth shall make you free. Therefore if the Son makes you free, you shall be free indeed" (John 8:32, 36 NKJV).

These were all difficult skills to acquire and to incorporate into my life, but they are skills that I am learning in my late sixties. Whoever said an old dog cannot learn new tricks? I'm not as far along on some areas as I am on others, and they definitely require someone to provide feedback and keep me focused. Gaining the victory in previously troublesome spots brings great satisfaction and joy.

In March 2014, I was driving 225 miles to sit with a dying friend. I stayed with her for two weeks, day and night, and was holding her hand as she entered heaven. On the way home, I was pondering the exchange that had just taken place: an earthly body and home for a heavenly body and home. Then I began to think of the many exchanges that God has worked in my life, which was the inspiration for this poem:

Exchange
He gave new life when I was dead.
When I was starved, became my bread.
There was no path, became my way.
When all was night, brought brilliant day.
I couldn't walk—He gave me wings.
To barren hearts, all gifts He brings.
From battles lost, became my shield.
From hardened heart, to Him I yield.
To bubbling springs, from deserts dry.
To weep with joy, from tearless eye.
From barren waste, to gushing streams.
From wooden hearts, to visions, dreams.
From garden dry, to pouring rain.
To comfort sweet, from endless pain.
To breath and life, from dusk and gloom.
From trash and weed, to bud and bloom.

Endless Waves of Grace

"For I know the plans I have for you," declares the Lord, "plans to prosper you and not to harm you, plans to give you hope and a future. Then you will call upon me and come and pray to me, and I will listen to you. You will seek me and find me when you seek me with all your heart. I will be found by

you," declares the Lord, "and will bring you back from captivity" (Jeremiah
29:11–14a).

I am learning to pray scripture. For these verses, I would pray something
like this: "Thank You, Lord, for having plans just for me. Thank You for
Your plans that will help me and bring hope to me. Thank You that You
hear me when I pray. You actually listen to me. And I never knew I could
really find You. When I give You all my heart, will You really set me free?
You said you will bring me back from my captivity. Thank You. It seems
that my whole life has been caught in a trap, but I believe You will deliver
me. Thank You, Jesus." God honors His Word. He desires that we would
believe it. Any step we take in that direction will bring a positive response
from Him.

Of all the poems I have written, "Like a Hound" is my favorite. As far
back as I can remember, I've known the Twenty-Third Psalm, but only for
the past year have I recognized how true its words have been in my life.
God's goodness is always present; I can never escape His love (Romans
8:38–39). I have the firm assurance that His mercy and grace not only
follow me but literally pursue me. The following poem illustrates this
conviction:

Like a Hound
*"Surely goodness and mercy shall follow me all the days of my life:
and I will dwell in the house of the Lord forever" Psalm 23:6.*
Something's behind me,
Pursuing me home,
Pushing me hard all the way:
Goodness and mercy,
God's grace and His love,
Helping me make it today.

What is following me?
What's hard on my heels?
I look back to see it behind:
Goodness and mercy,
God's joy and His peace,
To assure me that I'm on His mind.

Like a hound on a trail,
He's letting me know
That I'm never alone on the road;
Goodness and mercy
Are chasing me down,
Helping me carry the load.

In all of the places that I've ever been,
Through all my days,
Short or long,
Goodness and mercy
Have tracked after me,
Giving me hope and a song.

There'll not be a day
They won't be behind
Flaunting God's loving embrace:
Goodness and mercy,
All the way home,
Goodness and mercy and grace.

Philippians 1:6 (TLB) reads, "And I am sure that God who began the good work within you will keep right on helping you grow in his grace until his task within you is finally finished on that day when Jesus Christ returns."

Romans 5:1–2 (TLB) has encouraged me, too, for it says, "So now, since we have been made right in God's sight by faith in his promises, we can have real peace with him because of what Jesus Christ our Lord has done for us. For because of our faith, he has brought us into this place of highest privilege where we now stand, and we confidently and joyfully look forward to actually becoming all that God has had in mind for us to be."

God can and does redeem. He has no limits. There is hope! This hope is in God's grace, which always beats against our shores, in order to reach our cries and needs.

Endless waves of grace.

Notes

This is the journal entry about the emotional side of Pastor Bill's abuse, which I referred to in chapter 6.

Journal, August 26, 2014
Pastor Bill wanted me with him all the time. I had no life of my own—I was just an extension of his. Every day he would approach me sexually. He'd lock the doors first, which gave me a few seconds to escape (disassociate), time enough to freeze, then smile. He would often have been studying for a sermon or class. The Bible would be open on his desk. How could he switch so quickly? That's how I knew I was nothing more than a physical thing to him. He didn't consider me a person. I was a thing, just a vagina.

When we would be somewhere together, quite often someone would recognize him. He would lie, saying he had students with him and that we had either been somewhere or were going somewhere. I would think, *Help me. I'm being abducted,* but I never said a word. He would buy things for me. Only once, I would not take his gift. My refusal made him very angry. I was afraid of his anger, but every time I did accept anything, I thought of myself as a prostitute.

When I got to Minnesota, I was already so little. Being forced to do what I detested, and be what I wasn't, broke me further. The small pieces of me were broken into even smaller pieces. Many of the pieces were ground into powder and lost. I was as broken as if I had been run through a stone crusher. I was nothing. I was gone. I equaled zero. How many pieces could I find of me? None. I had nothing to begin the rebuilding process. I finally understand why, for thirty years, I couldn't respond to the people who wanted to help me. So many were friendly and thoughtful, but I didn't have anything to work with, no material with which to start rebuilding. I had lost myself. [Later, therapists constructed "blocks," and I could begin rebuilding my life.]

Such relentless condemnation while I was standing in front of the students and teaching! Where I had just been was so vivid in my mind. I was humiliated because some or all of the other students surely knew what I had been doing. Much, much, much, much worse was the knowledge that God knew. What could I pray? I was sure that the only One who could help me wouldn't help me. I made my bed—now I needed to lie in it.

Pastor Bill's touch gave me the creeps. It was never a touch of love or care. It was like a lion snapping a gazelle's neck and breaking it so he could devour it. Every sexual touch pulled something from me. I became less and less. Even when nothing was there, he could still pull out more. How could he continue to do that, when after a while, there was nothing?

Then he'd preach and pray. Sometimes the students would witness on the streets. He would always get one or two people to pray with him for salvation. To me, that was *proof* that he was right with God. So where did that put me? I must be the wrong one.

From the time I woke up in the morning until I went to bed at night, I was consumed with guilt and shame. *Oh, God, have mercy. Oh, God, have mercy. Oh, God, have mercy.* What else could I pray? I knew I would die there, and, after death, I'd go to hell.

It is impossible to describe how frightened I was. I couldn't have had more terror if a gunman pointed his gun at my head and cocked it. When he broke my finger, I finally realized how dangerous and unpredictable and tenuous my situation was. I never knew what would happen during the next hour. I would have thought that my early years would have made me immune to unpredictability. Can't someone get used to it? If it is normal, why should it still do such weird things to the brain? I know it wasn't truly *normal*, but since it was the regular daily situation, wouldn't it *seem* normal? And if it *seemed* normal, what told the brain to respond in such *abnormal* ways?

And now God! What was I to think about Him? I knew what I was supposed to believe. Hundreds of Bible verses talk of His love, joy, peace, forgiveness, mercy, grace, etc. But I didn't believe any of that for myself. It seemed that I was left on my own, to make it through life or not, to live or die.

I was so ashamed of my weakness. When Pastor Bill wouldn't talk to me, I would determine to hold out until he gave up and would acknowledge me again. Every time, I would resolve to maintain the silence, but I never could. He never gave up. He always won. I hated my weakness and inability to stand strong. I always went back to him. The only way he would accept me was if I initiated the sex. In a few minutes, I would be in good standing with him again, but I'd be in bad standing with God and with myself. I felt condemned because I always chose Pastor Bill instead of God. I always did what Pastor Bill wanted instead of what God wanted.

I don't know what I became. I shrunk down to nothing, and that nothing hid. Nothing real was present anymore. I was a Halloween costume, walking around but not real. Talking even, but the costume said what the person inside—Pastor Bill—wanted the costume to say. The true inside of the costume was gone, and Pastor Bill was there instead.

At this point, August 26, 2014, I can clearly see how God helped me all along. To save my life, He made me a good actor. I could disassociate and hide in my red-brick building. He not only got me through; He got me out.

Today was the first day I realized what was happening inside of me during the Bible school years. Pastor Bill's abuse began forty-one years ago, and only now am I able to begin processing it. I think the opening of feelings is good and healthy, but it's sad, too. It's only since I have written *Endless Waves* that I am not afraid anymore. I have no more guilt or shame or condemnation. But I do have some strong feelings today. I don't know exactly what. It's a little like sadness. I feel wounded and raw. I hurt. I want to cry.

I had assumed that thinking about this so much would be depressing. It isn't. It is clarifying. It's cleansing. It's like sweeping the floor. Dirt and trash were swept from my mind and spirit this morning.

Thanks be to God. Thanks be to God for His continuing work of grace.

Bibliography

Allender, Dan B. *The Wounded Heart*. Colorado Springs: NavPress, 2008.

Bass, Ellen and Laura Davis. *The Courage to Heal: A Guide for Women Survivors of Child Sexual Abuse*. New York: Harper & Row, 1988.

Chapman, Gary. *The Five Love Languages*. Chicago: Northfield Publishing, 2004.

Cloud, Henry and John Townsend. *Boundaries*. Grand Rapids: Zondervan, 1992.

Ferree, Marnie. *No Stones—Women Redeemed from Sexual Addiction*. Downers Grove: IVP Books, 2010.

Goleman, Daniel. *Social Intelligence*. New York: Bantam Books, 1997.

Hawthorne, Nathanial. *The Scarlet Letter*. Boston: Eldritch Press, 1850.

Perry, Bruce. *The Boy Who Was Raised as a Dog*. New York: Basic Books, 2006.

Contact

To contact the author, Nancy Kruithof O'Farrell, visit her website at www.endlesswaves.org or e-mail nancy@endlesswaves.org.